FIELD SPORTS
An Introduction

FIELD SPORTS
An Introduction

Jack Charlton and Tony Jackson

Based on the Channel Four Series 'Jack's Game'

Stanley Paul

London Melbourne Sydney Auckland Johannesburg

In association with
Channel Four Television Company Limited
and Yorkshire Television Limited

Stanley Paul & Co. Ltd
An imprint of the Hutchinson Publishing Group
17–21 Conway Street, London W1P 6JD

Hutchinson Group (Australia) Pty Ltd
PO Box 496, 16–22 Church Street,
Hawthorne, Melbourne, Victoria, 3122

Hutchinson Group (NZ) Ltd
32–34 View Road, PO Box 40–086, Glenfield,
Auckland 10

Hutchinson Group (SA) (Pty) Ltd
PO Box 337, Bergvlei 2012, South Africa

First published 1984
Reprinted 1984

Set in Linotron Ehrhardt by Tradespools Ltd,
Frome, Somerset

Printed and bound by Butler & Tanner Ltd,
Frome, Somerset

ISBN 0 09 155151 X

CONTENTS

ACKNOWLEDGEMENTS

For permission to reproduce photographs included in this book, the publisher and authors would like to thank Eric Begbie, Bord Failte (Irish Tourist Board), G.L. Carlisle, R.V. Collier, D.N. Dalton, John Darling, D. Doble, Ian A. Grindy, Pamela Harrison, John Marchington, Jim Meads, Steve Miller, John M. Morgan, Stuart Newsham, Roy Parker, Tom Parker, Roy Shaw, Dave Smyth, Graham Swanson, John Tarlton, John Walton, Robin Williams, Yorkshire Television. The Yorkshire Television photographs were taken by Brian Cleasby.

The chapter on pigeon shooting is based on Archie Coats's book *Pigeon Shooting*, edited by Colin Willock – reproduced by kind permission of the publishers Andre Deutsch.

Rough shooting

INTRODUCTION

Jack Charlton

Whether it's football, whether it's working the dog for a hedgerow pheasant or ferreting for rabbits on a frosty morning, I don't mind admitting I enjoy the game – and I work hard at it.

Finding out more about field sports for this book and the TV programme has been a real pleasure for me. Working with the experts has shown me just how much there is to learn, and what a grand time you can have learning it. We've been all over the country, in every kind of weather. We've been to Scotland for some wildfowling and to the Highlands stalking deer. I've learned how to build a hide for pigeon shooting and driven grouse across a grouse moor not long after 'the Glorious Twelfth'. Hunt followers may be disappointed to find fox hunting isn't covered here, but I'd have to learn to ride a horse before I could tackle that particular field sport, I'm afraid!

'Country sports make us observant and bring us closer to nature,' says Fred Taylor, and I'll go along with that. The more we learn about the countryside, the more we respect it. Thankfully, strict codes of practice govern field sports today, and critics of 'hunting, shooting and fishing' have no need to fear for the survival of our wildlife. Thanks to the rules and regulations in this country, we have thriving populations of game, and wildfowl and deer are actually on the increase.

My thanks to all nine experts for their advice and friendship during the past months. I hope the reader will enjoy discovering country sports as much as I have, and find just as much satisfaction in the field.

Pause for a flask on a cold morning's ferreting

FERRETING

Fred J. Taylor

Hunting rabbits with the aid of ferrets may be regarded solely as an effective method of pest control, but it is also a rural sport which has been practised in this country for centuries. In its simplest form it involves releasing a ferret into a rabbit bury, burrow or warren to flush out the residents into previously set nets or in front of waiting guns. Thus it is possible, in an ideal situation, to set – say – three nets over a total of three holes, release a ferret and, with luck, catch a brace of rabbits. I have done it many times, but, as with all sporting activity, there is a lot more to ferreting than the basic technique.

Although it is possible to get started with a minimum of expense and delay (subject to landowners' permission), it has to be remembered that ferreting is an all-year-round exercise which involves the nonstop care of and attention to livestock and equipment.

It may be fairly reckoned that the first requirement is a ferret, but, in fact, a large, airy, secure hutch stands firmly in the number one slot. Only then can stock be considered.

What stock to acquire depends upon the amount of rabbiting available, but I do not believe it is possible to do any serious ferreting without at least two jills (females) and a strong hob (male). The jills run loose, whereas the hob works on a line or with an electronic aid (of which more later) and will have to learn to accept a collar. Most ferrets hunt naturally and need no training but all have to be handled and 'gentled'

at an early age. Most young ferrets bite at some time or other but, with handling and good care, that problem is usually solved within a week.

There will almost certainly be a Ferret Welfare Society group within a phone call's distance of most homes and before purchasing stock it is advisable to contact that body for advice, which will be freely given.

Once you have acquired your ferrets, the more time that can be devoted to the animals, the better they will be in the field. I cannot stress this point too strongly. Ferrets should be handled, stroked, petted, talked to, and generally inspected daily. They are the most interesting of creatures and have characters of their own. Let no one fool you into believing that they are spiteful, nasty, vicious or untrustworthy, or that the ferret which doesn't bite is a poor hunter. Do not heed the know-all who insists that you have to be tough and rough with ferrets. Do not believe those who tell you that it is essential to muzzle them. It is not. It is, however, essential to develop a good relationship, and the prime factor for a good relationship between a ferret and its owner is cleanliness. Clean animals will remain healthy, work well and give offence to no one.

Quarters must be waterproof, draughtproof and airy. They should be warm in winter and cool in summer. Ferrets suffer in heat and metal-topped hutches are bad. Asbestos or some kind of cavity insulation in a plain wooden roof is better. Sleeping quarters may be enclosed and separate from the main run, but this is not essential. If you are fortunate enough to have an unused shed which is vermin proof and has a window, you have an ideal home for a bunch of happy ferrets. Toss a few pieces of pipe inside (land drain sections are ideal), litter the floor with hay or straw, toss in a couple of full bales and let them have fun sorting out their own quarters. This, in my opinion, and with one reservation, is the finest way to keep ferrets and the most interesting from an onlooker's point of view. The reservation is that working hobs ought to be separated from their jills. A hob that lives with his ladies all year round will not be so keen to seek them out in the field. This, as will be explained later, is the hob's job.

Special care and some patience may be needed to quieten down newly bought stock. First-year youngsters, though a bit wild at first, are quick to respond. A ferret that has been sent by rail and has endured long hours in the confines of a small box is likely to be temperamental when released. It should not be snatched from its box. It makes sense to open the box inside the new quarters, feed the ferret, give it a drink of milk and, after it has settled, begin to handle it. You may be bitten for your pains, but the bite will not be serious! Close your fist and let the ferret sniff the hard knuckle part. If it decides to bite, it can do no harm except break the skin. Do not snatch your hand away; instead, push it towards the ferret. Pick it up quietly and carefully behind the neck and front legs with your other hand and begin to make friends with it. I doubt if you will ever be bitten more than once and if you really make a fuss of it, it will come eagerly onto your outstretched palm within a few days.

Having good, quiet, reliable stock is vital to good ferreting and these are the first steps towards that end.

FEEDING

Feeding is, of course, equally important and, without going too deeply into the subject of diet, it is fair to say that ferrets will grow strong and remain healthy on a meat and water diet. Liver should not be fed more than once a week and the occasional meal of bread and milk or raw fish will provide variety. Water should be changed daily and sleeping quarters inspected for hidden remnants. Ferrets almost invariably take surplus food to the 'bedroom' and hide it; it is advisable to watch closely and avoid overfeeding.

Always call in advance at feed time and you will find the ferrets waiting for you when you arrive.

EQUIPMENT

Having settled the problems of stock and living quarters, it now becomes necessary to consider other items of equipment needed for work in the field. It can be an expensive business, but it pays to buy the best at the outset. I believe that if you enter into the true spirit of ferreting it must be with no thought of profit in mind. (Today, I understand, rabbits fetch about £1 apiece. I never sold one so I do not know.)

Purse nets, for setting over each open hole, may cost up to £1.20 each, food is expensive, so too is petrol, and I do not believe it is possible for two operators to do more than break even over a season's rabbiting. My partner and I keep and tend (at present) a dozen ferrets. We feed them meat, we buy hay and straw, and we have some 200 purse nets which are probably worth £200. An electronic unit – which is hardly ever used – costs, with spare collars, around £40. The gate net and a 25-yard long-net, both of which are essential to our kind of ferreting, can possibly be disregarded by a beginner, but the cost of carrying bags, lines, collars, extra food when youngsters are bred, the occasional vet's fee, and a good graft or spade adds up to a fair sum.

Ferreting is a sporting exercise, however, and it is possible to build up stocks of equipment over a long period. To be utterly practical, a modest start may be made with – say – a dozen purse nets, a line, a collar, a carrying bag or box and an ordinary garden spade. A sharp penknife for gutting and legging rabbits is necessary, and a pair of secateurs for cutting away briars and brambles in the field is extremely useful. It might just be possible to make a start, using existing

Ferret – an intelligent, courageous and clean animal

equipment, for an outlay of about £25. It will, however, cost more as time goes by and the need for more gear becomes apparent.

It is vital to ensure that carrying bags or boxes are completely secure. Ferrets are incredible escapologists!

WORKING

In the meantime, let us go back to field basics once more. They are very simple, but require silence and caution.

Purse nets are put over all the holes in the rabbit bury, loose jill ferrets are released to hunt underground and, with luck, rabbits bolt into the waiting nets where they are quickly ensnared and dispatched.

A net should be set so that the retaining peg allows the mesh to cover the hole. There are no set rules, but it makes sense to try to ensure that a bolting rabbit hits the centre of the mesh. While ferrets are working underground it is advisable always to avoid standing directly in front of any of the holes. Cautious rabbits, intending to slip away quietly, will see that all is not well and change their minds. They will then face the ferrets rather than bolt, and the result will be a long delay until they are trapped or killed underground. This will cause even longer delays since they have to be recovered by digging. So if possible always stand downwind of the bury while the jills are hunting, and do not smoke or talk.

It may take a pair of jills a long time to locate rabbits in all but the smallest of buries, so do not be impatient. Give them time.

Young, inexperienced ferrets may behave a little irrationally at the outset. They may run from hole to hole, pulling nets aside as they do so. They may be reluctant to return to hand for the first few days, but they will settle eventually. Soon they will learn to slip through a net mesh without disturbing it, and it will not take them long to discover that they achieve little by running around above ground.

It is always worrying when young ferrets stay down for long periods. It is even more worrying when older jills do so. Mature jills can kill, and there are times when they will appear to be completely 'laid-up', but it is always worth waiting quietly for at least an hour before taking further action.

If, after a suitable period of waiting, it is obvious that the rabbits are not going to bolt, you can put the hob to work on a line. A good length is about 7 yards. Attach his collar, making sure he cannot pull his head through it and tease a little of his fur forward in front of the collar as an extra precaution.

It is fairly safe to assume that a hob ferret will locate a jill underground. He is more likely to do so if he has had no female companion, which is the reason for keeping hob liners and loose jills in separate hutches. The prime function of a line ferret is to push loose jills off a kill, or off a rabbit which, for some reason, they are unable to budge. Generally speaking, in buries of reasonable size, the liner takes over and the jills quickly return to hand above ground. If two jills are on the same kill, both will come back at once. If they are on separate kills, they will have to be located individually. This can cause problems at times.

In order to retrieve the kill, it is necessary to dig down to the line ferret by following the path of the line, but when two jills are working it must be remembered that they may not be together. It is extremely important to keep all tunnels open during the dig in order not to trap the second jill.

She could be anywhere, and in a maze of tunnels it is easy to block off her escape.

Some ferreters refer to the business of following the line as 'crowning down', others refer to it as 'breaking in', but, whatever name it goes by, following the line to the hob ferret and his kill (ideally after the jills have returned above ground, but if not you can be fairly confident that they are sharing the kill with the liner) involves a number of digs to locate the line at various stages. By poking a flexible stick along the hole for as far as possible and breaking in at that point, it is fairly simple to find the line, get another angle of direction with the same stick and repeat the procedure. Knowing the exact length of the line will help you work out how far the hob ferret has advanced (some ferreters mark their lines at 1-yard intervals) and, by breaking in with the spade, locating the line and following its path, you will eventually locate the kill. Sometimes all the ferrets will be found together, but if jills have split up and are with different kills the procedure has to be repeated.

The modern electronic unit, though possibly less sporting, does away with multiple digs since the receiver unit above ground pinpoints the hob's electronic collar quickly and accurately. In these circumstances, and provided the electronics are utterly reliable, the line may be dispensed with entirely. Many modern ferreters no longer bother with a line but rely instead on the electronic collar and hand-held receiver. Whether you decide to use one is up to you. It will certainly make digging easier in most situations but there may be times when it is not quite as easy as it all seems, as we shall see. I am not against these devices. I have two of them, but I seldom need to use them. On the rare occasions when I use a big hob ferret with an electronic collar, I keep him on a line just in case things go wrong.

As I have already pointed out, a good line ferret will stay with the kill until he is reached by digging. Not all hob ferrets are good stayers, however, and it may be as well to discuss the selection of a line ferret at this stage.

When hob ferrets are young and inexperienced, they may be worked loose in the same way

Young ferrets in their nest

as jills. They will bolt rabbits quite naturally and come to hand when no quarry is left underground. At some point, however, there will come a time when one of the young hobs stays with a rabbit and steadfastly refuses to budge. At that particular moment he will present a problem, but he will be a future line ferret and his education should begin. Choose small buries if possible when training your first liner, and introduce him to the collar at once.

Line ferrets can, of course, be worked in small buries without the aid of jills and, in these circumstances, there is no real reason why a hob should not work loose with a transmitter collar attached. Where buries are very deep, however, it is unwise to allow a strong hob to run loose — even with the aid of electronics. He may kill in a very deep part of the complex, completely out of receiver range, and be impossible to retrieve with ordinary digging equipment. He will return above ground eventually unless he is prevented from doing so by circumstances over which he has no control, but the waiting can be time-consuming and frustrating. Very big complexes are best left strictly alone unless there are plenty of loose ferrets and willing workers available. Even then work should begin on them as early in the day as possible. They should not be considered late in the morning since lie-ups and long waits are extremely likely.

There are times when jill ferrets lie up underground and for some reason cannot be located by a searching hob. Generally speaking this happens when a rabbit is killed or backed up in a dead end. The frustrated jill ferret refuses to leave her quarry but can do little more than scratch upon its rear end. Rabbits learn quickly, however, that bunching up in a dead end, though

unpleasant at the time, serves to protect them adequately from ferrets and other natural enemies. A bald patch is about the only indignity they suffer, and a rabbit that has once escaped in this way will try the dodge again. Waiting for a jill ferret to return is annoying and at such times it is advisable to locate her with a lined hob and move on elsewhere.

There are also occasions, however, when a jill becomes trapped between two dead rabbits or in a dead end that is blocked by the body of a rabbit killed by another hunting ferret. The only escape route is via a rabbit corpse that has to be eaten through. Mature ferrets can kill rabbits extremely quickly by biting the jugular vein and, being keen hunters, they are apt to move on in search of more quarry. One ferret's kill may trap another in a tight situation. If a line hob will not

Entering a polecat ferret into a netted hole

stay with the corpse (and some will not), it may be necessary to wait until dark in the hope that the jill will find her own way back above ground.

If, when darkness falls, she is still underground, it becomes necessary to contain her overnight. Holes have to be blocked with turves (but not filled in) and an early morning return planned. Placing a bundle of hay or straw at one entrance and baiting it with a piece of rabbit liver often sees the lost jill fast asleep and none the worse for wear next morning. In more serious lie-up situations, it may be necessary to return several times before the lost creature comes to light. Sometimes, unfortunately, ferrets are lost for ever and often the reason for the loss is never quite understood. I am convinced, however, that in the great majority of cases it is due to circumstances beyond the ferret's control.

Sometimes, mid-day hold-ups can be dealt with by gutting a previously caught rabbit and placing the entrails in front of one of the holes so that the scent drifts into the main complex. Wind direction is a consideration here, of course, and there are times when the ploy works like sheer magic. Alas, there are others when it is a dismal failure! Losing the odd ferret is part of the game, however, and while it is sad to have to write off a good worker, it has to be accepted as inevitable at times.

It goes without saying that permission to hunt rabbits must be obtained from the land owner before ferrets can be worked and, having obtained that permission, it becomes essential to understand rabbit 'signs'. Rabbit holes may be easy to find but there is never any guarantee that they are occupied. General signs are flattened grass or nettles around the holes, fresh droppings in the vicinity, fresh scratchings, well-worn entrances, and often a rabbit smell. Signs that holes are *not* used are cobwebs, weeds and grass or piles of dry leaves in the entrances, and a generally overgrown appearance.

Accepted signs do not always live up to their reputations, however, and buries showing all the signs of occupation can sometimes be vacant. Likewise, obviously empty buries may well contain an odd refugee. Nothing is ever certain, but it is often possible to get some idea of the situation by allowing a tethered hob ferret to sniff around the entrance holes. Most hobs have a good sense of smell and if one shows no enthusiasm after inspecting each hole separately, there is not much point in netting up and proceeding. If, however, the hob shows excitement and is keen to proceed, he should be restrained and the complex netted. Absolute silence is essential in these circumstances, as indeed it is in all ferreting operations. Noise can deter rabbits from bolting and the sporting aspect is lost if the end result is a dismal dig.

Where rabbits are concentrated in thick hedgerow cover, it is almost impossible to work without causing some kind of disturbance, and a decision has to be made as to what constitutes the best working procedure. There are several alternatives. The first one is to crash in, net up all the holes and hope for the best. Sometimes it works and the rabbits cooperate by bolting. More often than not, however, they sense trouble above ground and stay put. In a situation such as this, many operators tend to block off most of the holes with turves and go to work with a line ferret, accepting from the outset that digging will be necessary.

By netting all the readily accessible holes, and leaving those in the thick cover strictly alone, it is often possible to encourage rabbits to bolt. It is a common practice for rabbits to go from one hole to another when taking evasive action, and it is not at all unusual for one to vacate via an unnetted hole and be caught trying to go down another. This is referred to as back-netting, and very often the only indication that it has happened is the sight of a taut draw string disappearing underground.

There are times when it pays to clear away cover and make the holes accessible several days before putting the ferrets to work. This can be done with secateurs and need not be drastic. The only requirement is sufficient room to place nets over all the holes without undue noise. Rabbits may be discouraged for a day or so by this action but, generally speaking, they are soon back in residence.

In extreme circumstances, large and badly overgrown complexes may be dealt with by a 'stinking-out' process. The object is to move the occupants from a difficult situation to one which is smaller and easier to work. Obviously some nearby quarters are essential. There is no point in stinking-out rabbits if they are likely to vacate the territory altogether, but when they are driven from one set of holes, rabbits will almost invariably take up residence in the next available complex. This results in overcrowding, and rabbits in overcrowded conditions may be relied upon to bolt quickly when ferrets are introduced.

Stinking-out is done with sheets of newspaper soaked in creosote and loosely rolled into balls. These are pushed as far down the holes as possible, leaving only two or three as escape avenues. Rabbits do not care for the smell of tar or creosote and will usually vacate overnight. Then it is a simple matter, a couple of days later, to ferret the nearby, smaller complexes and reap a handsome reward.

Those are the main alternatives available to the operator faced with difficult or near-impossible situations; the choice is up to the individual after due consideration.

Only one other strategy remains – attempting to bolt the rabbits in front of strategically placed guns. From the point of view of sheer efficiency, I would not choose to shoot over ferrets at all, since I regard it very much as a hit-and-miss exercise! Nevertheless, there is something to be said for the sporting aspect, although there are limitations and many rabbits will escape. In thick cover, chances of sporting shots are not too high, and bolting rabbits tend to stay close to cover. A clean break across open meadowland seldom occurs and most shots have to be executed quickly. Rabbits may show themselves long enough to get themselves killed, but they still have nasty habits of kicking themselves into deep ditches, thick cover or nearby holes. They then have to be located and picked up, all of which causes a disturbance over the area which has still to be worked. Dogs seeking lost rabbits undoubtedly deter other rabbits from bolting and cause delays and lie-ups. Boltholes can be overlooked, rabbits in cover may sneak quietly out of a hole in the middle of the hedgerow and proceed cautiously away from the hunting ferrets. I have often found myself face to face with a startled rabbit making a leisurely escape along a double hedge where I have been lying prone to cover a possible escape route.

Despite the drawbacks, however, shooting over ferrets can be organized into a sport that is safe and enjoyable to all concerned. It is better for one participant to do nothing more than handle and work the ferrets; it is unwise to try to work ferrets and shoot at the same time. I have tried it often enough but I have never been truly happy about it.

Organized shooting at bolted rabbits has to be considered in advance. Guns have to be deployed safely and with due regard to the path most likely to be taken by bolting rabbits. That, in itself, is very difficult to assess but it is all part of the sport of ferreting. They should be placed out of line with the holes being worked and with due consideration to wind direction. Rabbits have a good sense of smell and are very much aware of movement. The sudden appearance of a rabbit at a hole may cause guns to mount prematurely, with the result that the rabbit goes back underground. It is difficult for a shooting man not to react to such happenings, but it really does pay to wait until a clean break is made. That way rabbits are killed away from the bury where they may be retrieved without affecting the hunt that is still taking place. Rabbits taken leisurely and away from the main set are also fit to dress out and eat. Those taken too quickly usually end up as mangled carcases unfit to eat.

Shooting over ferrets also offers a good opportunity to work young and inexperienced stock by giving them a chance to settle down and become steadier in the field. Young ferrets are usually very keen to work and their frantic and excited excursions from hole to hole sometimes make it difficult to keep purse nets correctly set. There is a lot to be said for standing back quietly and letting young animals do their own thing. The noise made by guns, for some reason, does not seem to deter bolting rabbits. Footsteps and activity on the bury often does.

There is no doubt a great deal more to the sport of ferreting than has been outlined here, and there are certain aspects of it which have to

End of a morning's ferreting

be learned through sheer experience. I have never stopped learning; I doubt I ever will. If I did, I know that my own sporting pleasures would be diminished and that, as a result, I would lose interest. All country sports make us observant and bring us closer to nature. We learn to reap the harvests that come each year and we learn that overexploitation makes no sense at all. And that is as true of ferreting as of any other countryside activity.

19

Jack and Archie Coats at the end of a successful shoot

PIGEON SHOOTING

Archie Coats

This chapter is for all pigeon shooters: for the young, who may well find that shooting woodpigeon gives them as much pleasure as shooting any other game; and for the serious pigeon shooter, who will probably have to think of the financial side, as I do. The combination of first-class sport with the destruction of a costly pest sounds attractive, but, as with anything else, there is a right and a wrong way to go about it. So I hope that my advice will help you obtain better sport and put more pigeons in your bag. Don't blame me if one day you find yourself half a mile from your car, with 150 wet pigeons to carry across three very soggy ploughed fields.

Pigeon shooting is first and foremost a 'do-it-yourself' game, and for this reason is more fun than more organized sports. It has given me great satisfaction to know that I have helped a lot of people discover shooting, and provided a little know-how through lectures, game fairs and my book, *Pigeon Shooting* (André Deutsch), on which this chapter is based.

Columba palumbus, the ring-necked dove or woodpigeon, does a vast amount of harm to the farming fraternity, as well as eating all the green stuff in your back garden as a sideline. Nevertheless, I am very fond of the woodpigeon, although I make my living out of its destruction. The 'woody', as it is sometimes called, goes by other names as well. Most of them are unprintable, but in my native Ayrshire we used to call them

'cushat', 'cushy doo' or simply 'doo'. The Welsh call them 'queest' or 'quist'.

The woody makes a rather flat, flimsy nest of enlaced twigs in any thickish bush or tree, not usually more than 20 feet from the ground. Secondary growth or mixed forestry plantations are its favourite nesting habitat, the chosen site always being near a feeding area and water supply.

Incubation of the eggs lasts about seventeen days, with both birds taking turns at sitting; if one parent is killed, the other will carry on. I have often wondered whether a foster parent takes over the job of incubation, or at least feeds the young, if both parents are killed, but I have no proof of this. The young stay in the nest for about three weeks, and for the first few days are fed, by both parents, on 'pigeon's milk'. This is a cheese-like liquid which is regurgitated by the parent when the youngster inserts its soft, shovel-like beak into the parent's throat. Gradually the youngster's diet is extended to include partly digested grain, which is full of protein. It is perhaps because of this that squabs hatched late in the season survive better than those hatched earlier on, when the parent birds are eating kale and other less nutritive food.

Most of the youngsters do not fly until late August or September, by which time the harvest is usually over. Towards the end of September and particularly in October, the young birds flock together and move about the country gleaning from the stubble. Then, by way of a one-year ley, they learn that clover and rape taste good too. It is these packs of first-year birds that probably are the basis for the stories of the thousands of migratory birds ('they furriners') which are supposed to visit these shores. In fact, there are very few pigeons in Europe compared with this country. Why should there be an export market from the UK to Europe if the locals could meet their own demand?

Archie Coats – the professional. 'A man who spends his life outwitting pigeon'

There are three other species of wild pigeons or doves resident in Britain. The stock dove is descended from the cage birds kept by monks for culinary purposes. They make better eating than ring-necks, particularly in winter, but shooting them is now banned by EEC regulations, quite unnecessarily, in my opinion. The almost identical rock dove, often of a slightly lighter colour, is a bird of the wild coasts and cliffs. They never sit in trees, but I have seen them on the stooked oats in Islay, and no doubt they could be decoyed. The collared dove, which has recently established itself as a breeding resident, has not yet reached pest proportions. It is now off the protected list and makes a nuisance of itself taking pheasant feed and grain stored in barns. The turtle dove, a migrant which comes here to nest, is on the protected list. It is a charming little bird and, apart from eating small amounts of grain from time to time, is not destructive.

Modern forestry practice favours the wood-pigeon by providing nesting and roosting cover. However, the bird prefers strips, parkland and small spinneys to the dense mass of great woods. This is probably because it is basically a lazy creature and likes its home to be fairly close to the restaurant so that it can fly to its chosen field without much effort. The woodpigeon prefers to feed in the open. Downland, with its strips and belts, is often the best game country and also harbours most pigeons. There is always what I call a good 'background' to a favourite pigeon area: by this I mean a number of woods or belts of trees which provide roosting and nesting cover in season and which the birds use as a base.

With a little practice you can soon learn to read a 1-inch map and spot the likely areas for woodpigeon. The contours are important, as these determine the line of flight. Pigeons rarely fly without a purpose, and their movements are usually dictated by their desire to be gregarious and eat together in one particular field. Although they move about the country from the middle of October until the end of April, they are nevertheless parochially minded once they settle down. They may travel some distance at this time of year, but once they decide your crops are to their liking, they stay put. They won't move away until the food gives out, or they decide that your neighbour's land has more to offer, or you make things too hot for them. The only time your locals, particularly the young birds, will leave you is in October. The worst time to have a visitation is at the end of March: if the weather is mild and the clover and rape good, or you are spring sowing, it is highly probable that they will be with you for the duration, so to speak.

Although the winter of 1962–63 decimated pigeon stocks, the number of birds has subsequently increased, but not to its former level. Pigeon damage in this country is well-nigh incalculable. An attempt has been made by the Game Conservancy at Fordingbridge to assess the cost, and it comes to many millions of pounds. A pigeon eats from 1000 to 1300 grains of wheat a day. In July and August this is one and a half cropfuls. A full crop weighs up to 3½ oz, which means that one bird consumes about 5 oz of wheat a day. It take 30 oz of wheat to make a 1½-lb loaf. Therefore in six days one pigeon eats the equivalent to an average loaf. It can also eat 800–1000 grains of malting quality barley in a day. Barley swells more than wheat, but the bird still gets through one and a half cropfuls in the summer, which weighs about 3–4 oz. It takes 3 oz of malting quality to make 1.18 pints of mild ale. Therefore, as the thirsty and envious will note, a pigeon can live, like the Latuka tribesmen in equatorial Sudan, in an alcoholic stupor for most of the summer. Foolish birds, they prefer wheat. However, nowadays you can also find them on rape stubble after harvest, and they can do considerable damage to a one-year ley. Lucerne, beans, seed rye grass, young kale and brassicas are all grist to the pigeon's mill. Winter and spring oil-seed rape and vining and seed peas now provide the bulk of my shooting. Some experts claim that a little mild grazing doesn't hurt, but I, and others, think that pigeon damage is never mild.

You don't need a game licence to shoot pigeons, but you must have a shotgun certificate. Although pigeons are classed as vermin, you cannot just go out and shoot them. You have to ask permission and this must be done with tact. The local keeper, if there is one, is the best bet, otherwise the farmer. Some sort of reference will help, the membership of a local club, for example. If you are given permission, treat the land as if it were your own. Don't leave gates open, tidy up your hide, shoot any vermin, but don't poke about in hedgerows (and don't let your dog do it either), especially in the nesting season. Decoying in a static pigeon hide does not disturb game; walking about does.

RECONNAISSANCE

There are two types of reconnaissance: the first is to find the restaurant field, and the second to select the correct place to site the hide. Almost everyone I take out wants to get cracking straightaway. This is understandable, but remember the old army manual precept that 'time spent on reconnaissance is never wasted'. It is a difficult lesson for the young to learn.

If you were to set me down at about 2 p.m. in any part-wooded, part-arable district of the United Kingdom, and I had a car, a 1-inch map of the area and a good pair of binoculars, I can guarantee to say whether there were any pigeon operating in the area and in due course find the field they were feeding in. After examining the field, I could tell you where to put the hide. This is not boasting, but a statement of fact; reconnaissance is the first vital step in successful decoying. It will help your case considerably if, when you approach a farmer for permission to shoot on his land, you can say, 'There are a lot of pigeons on your one-year ley by that old black barn.' So how do you set about finding them?

Woodpigeon landing. Enemy of farmers and gardeners

Remember, they are gregarious feeders; they enjoy eating together and keep to the one restaurant while the food and service are good. This charming though foolish habit is the cause of their downfall and makes decoying possible. What is more, they will return to that field after being shot at. Don't believe the cry: 'We had one shot and the —— never came back!' or the stories you read in the sporting press.

Knowing what their diet is likely to be at any time of year, and therefore what fields to look out for, is essential for reconnaissance. In summer this will take longer as the pigeons are spread out. Watch the lines of flight and where they converge – that will give you the answer. In winter, pigeons set off from their dormitories to feed at dawn. Only the cock pheasant and the crow beat them to it. Thereafter, in winter and early spring, they stay in the one field, or flight to it from another or from a line of trees which they use as a resting or preening place. So hungry are they that they feed virtually all day, the green stuff being rapidly digested.

HIDES AND HIDE SITING

Once you have established what field the pigeon is feeding in, the second essential for successful decoying is to site the hide correctly. Friends who have been out with me remark that I think like a pigeon – no one has yet said that I resemble one, but no doubt that will come. This is not so foolish as it sounds, for thinking like a pigeon means being able to create a natural picture, one which corresponds to what the bird expects to see as it flies into its chosen field to feed. This is my definition of decoying, and it applies all the year round, whatever the birds are eating. If you like, try to create this picture beside your favourite roosting wood or on a line of flight; it will prove beyond doubt that the pigeon is indeed so greedy and gregarious that it cannot bear to see Tom, Dick and Auntie Sue apparently eating their heads off, even on a most unlikely looking field, without joining them for a nightcap. Faith in the basic premise that pigeons will return to their chosen field and the careful building up of a picture to welcome them are the two most important keys to successful pigeon decoying. Everything else follows from that.

The pigeon is expecting to see a natural picture; this means that you must create it in the appropriate place. For some reason – perhaps depending on the line of flight, the direction of their home, the general background to the area, or the availability of good 'sitty' trees – pigeons seem to favour one specific location, for example, one side of a particular field. You must site your hide in that spot, under the main pigeon traffic. And once you have built your hide, always push the pigeons off the field *before* you start shooting.

Once you have chosen the site, you must decide on the type of hide suitable for the area. Hides fall into three categories:

(a) *Natural hides.* These are made out of existing bushes or vegetation, and you will need a hedgeknife or billhook. By far the best natural hide is made from the elder bush, which cuts and breaks easily. It can soon be shaped like a grouse butt, with about a 180-degree field of fire and suitable peepholes and background. Elder twigs, about 4–6 inches long, are ideal for sticking under the throats of slain birds when putting them out as decoys. Longer twigs can be used on posts and laid corn.

(b) *Artificial, portable hides.* Perhaps the best of these is made of two or three camouflage nets, set on pointed iron stakes. This hide is not really suitable for use in open country where it needs to be bushed up. Against an insubstantial background such as a wire fence, however, it works very well, and I use it increasingly, especially against or under a tree or hedge. It allows for sideways shots and solves the problem of overhang. Also, it enables you to learn to shoot from a sitting position, which gives you better angles and visibility.

(c) *The bale hide.* This is in a class of its own. Don't believe the old wives' tale that it has to be set up some days in advance for the pigeons to get used to it. You will have to ask the farmer to load at least thirteen bales on a trailer and take them out to the feeding area under the main pigeon traffic. Make the hide in the shape of a square, three bales up. This will take twelve bales, with the thirteenth as a seat. An extra bale can go at the back of your seat, as a fourth tier, to provide background if you stand up to shoot. The birds won't be able to see you so easily. Placing the bales on their side gives another 2 inches in height.

24

EQUIPMENT

You will need a fairly heavy billhook with a blade strong enough for a thickish branch. Also carry a pair of secateurs to clip away any annoying stalks or brambles. Use string or baling twine to tie back odd ends of branches which persist in falling in the wrong place. You will need a good amount of string if you are going to build a branch hide in the middle of a field. I use an empty 4–5 gallon oildrum to sit on, padding the seat with the sack in which I carry my billhook and dead pigeon decoys (a second sack for the dog to sit on is a good idea). The sharp rim of the oildrum can be uncomfortable to sit on, so I bang mine flat with a hammer, and this allows me to swivel more easily. Your gunslip must have a sling, and you can carry everything quite easily if you thread the sack with baling twine and tie it to the oildrum. Liquid sustenance, both for your-self and for your dog, contributes to happy pigeon shooting.

Personally, I don't think you can beat a double-barrel 12-bore, with improved cylinder in the right barrel for simple decoying shots, and half-choke in the left for going-away second shots and long shots. I use a side-by-side as I don't like the balance of an under-and-over for decoying. As for cartridges, there is none better than the No. 6 or No. 7 Eley Grand Prix for pigeon or game shooting.

SETTING OUT DECOYS

Setting out decoys and creating a natural picture is a fascinating game. In the winter months always keep a dozen or so dead pigeons back from the previous day's shoot. They keep quite well in winter, so there is no loss. In summer, however, it is a different story: you can't afford to

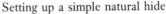

Setting up a simple natural hide

lose so many through blowflies. There are many artificial pigeons, wobblers and flappers, on the market. In my experience, artificials need to be covered with pigeon feathers. Set the dead birds out with a 4–6-inch stick under the chin. They should be 3 yards apart, no less.

Now study a flock of birds feeding undisturbed. They do not all face into the wind when feeding, and new arrivals often fly over their pals to the front of the line as if they were jumping the queue. The general tendency of the flock is to feed into the wind, but don't set your decoys out like a squad of guardsmen. The idea is to have one or two nice broad backs covering any angle of approach. This applies particularly if there is a tall tree or hedge nearby. The birds will think that Old Charlie has just dropped off the tree to feed. Cutting the eyelids off pigeons before you set them out is a waste of time, nor is it necessary to have all the decoys with their heads in the air

on sticks. Place some of them on the ground, or prop them up slightly on a bit of clover, for example. Again, look at an undisturbed flock. There are a few with their heads up, like sentries, but most of them are feeding. In this way you create the natural picture which is so important.

Pigeons usually land into the wind. Therefore site your decoys so that the incoming birds have to pass in front of the hide to reach the feeding area. I try to leave an empty space in the middle of my set-up. If the wind is behind you, site the decoys about 30–40 yards away from the hide, which is about the best pattern range for No. 6 or No. 7 shot. In adverse winds you may have to put them farther away and at different angles. It is a matter of trial and error. You need to cultivate a 'third eye' to tell you whether the pigeon you are preparing to fire at is your best chance. Use the lulls in pigeon traffic to build up and improve

Jack takes a woody over the decoys ...

... and quickly changes cartridges

your picture. It is like compound interest: the more you kill and put out, the better they come.

To attract the attention of passing pigeons which otherwise might not notice the decoys, keep one or two dead birds in the hide and lob or bowl them at hide height towards one which is in the open. Too much background may prevent passing pigeons from seeing the thrown decoy. This stratagem works very well from a hide under a single tree, as the pigeons presumably think that a bird has just flown down to feed. I have even used this ploy successfully from a bale hide. It doesn't always work, however; sometimes it seems to scare the daylights out of the birds. You will just have to experiment.

On many occasions you might have to force birds down to decoys in a field in which they are not actually feeding. You must create a picture which some of them will take as real, then build it up so that it becomes more attractive. The more decoys you start with the better – and the more accurate you are, the better still.

Shooting roosting birds is simple. You need to get to the roosting wood well before the birds come in, and reconnoitre to find the main roosting area, which is where most of the droppings are. Move 50 yards upwind and sit with your back to a tree or thick bush. Don't make a hide, but move when the line shows you where to go. Don't shoot too late into the evening, and pick up as you go along.

A different technique with roosting birds which can be most successful is to use one or two decoys up a tree. I don't bother with this myself, however, as I feel that getting on the line is sufficient. If the line changes, I don't want to be tied to a particular spot.

Another suggestion, for those who can only get off work at lunchtime on a Saturday, is to decoy just outside a roosting wood. This can give you a couple of hours' more shooting. Normally, roosting time only allows for an hour's shooting, but by getting there early you have a chance to get a few birds before they start roosting. Look out for tall ash trees or single beech trees. They are often used as 'sitty' trees before the birds go farther into the wood to roost. In the spring and summer, as the days grow longer and there is

Another pigeon in the bag

more time to feed, a few replete birds may come in early, but will be unable to resist joining their pals for a nightcap. A small wood is best, as the birds are more likely to see the decoys and your shot disturbs a larger area, setting up more birds.

Advanced decoying depends on what I call 'the power of the gun'. Start with as many decoys as possible, and whether you are shooting pigeons on acorns, beechmast, resting field, whatever the line of flight, you have to make a noise, relying on the birds to come upwind. You then shoot straight and keep building up your picture. Even decoys on a fallow field will bring a few birds in, although decoying on a ley is better.

It is not difficult, once you know the basic principles of decoying, to find a field and be successful. There will be times when nothing is obvious, although there are plenty of birds about. But on these occasions a little extra cunning, allied to local knowledge, will give you a great deal of fun and no little satisfaction.

Spying for a likely buck

ROE DEER STALKING

Richard Prior

Roe stalking in the early summer mornings is one of the most memorable pursuits. The woods are at their loveliest, and the birdsong, whether it be the dawn chorus of a South Country wood, or the bubbling call of a curlew and the challenges of grouse or blackcock loud on the fringe of the northern moors, is unforgettable. The sport is comparatively new in this country, but opportunities do exist, and if the chance comes up, it is one to grab with both hands. There is only one warning – once bitten with the roe-stalking bug, few devotees ever turn away from it. In terms of loss of sleep, travel, cost and generally anti-social behaviour, it is definitely not to be recommended!

If an experienced stalker invites you to go out, he will probably expect you to go down to the range when you arrive and have a few shots at a target. This is to check that your rifle is properly adjusted, or zeroed, so that the bullet and the aiming point coincide. This little session not only demonstrates to the stalker that you have gone to the trouble of trying your rifle to make sure that a properly aimed shot will result in a humane kill, but allows him to judge, to some extent, how difficult a shot he dare present you with. Humaneness to a living animal is always more important than achieving success for the visitor at any price. Remember the story about the visiting stalker who said that his gunmaker had just recently checked his rifle and nothing more was needed. 'Ah, sir,' said his stalker, 'but it was not the rifle that needed to be checked!' Most professional stalkers would never betray a confidence in this way, but the maximum enjoyment for all concerned starts with care and consideration for the quarry.

Next morning, the rendezvous is likely to be at an extremely early hour, maybe 4 or 5 a.m., so make sure that you have an alarm clock, several if you are a heavy sleeper, and that you know exactly where to meet the stalker. If necessary, get him to mark clearly on a map where you should meet, or agree on some landmark which can easily be found in the dark even though the country may be totally unfamiliar to you. Directions by someone who knows the country intimately are not necessarily straightforward to follow when, excited but still sleepy, you creep forth from the hotel. At this moment make sure, too, that you do not click the front door before you have assured yourself that the car keys are in your hand!

Do not be late at the appointed place as the first few minutes of daylight can be critical if an old buck is to be outwitted. Even if you arrive far too early, your guide will probably be there before you.

Long stalks as when hunting red deer in the Highlands are rare in roe stalking. Very often when a shootable beast does present itself, either it will already be in range or a few hurried moves will be needed to get you to the right position for a shot. Roe are nervous animals and a studied approach may bring you safely to the perfect spot, but not till the quarry has gone. This is, however, the only time when speed is of the essence. In passing through the woods, the pace has to be so slow and quiet as to be almost maddening to anyone used to more energetic pursuits. Even so, at the end of two or three hours' slow progress from one clearing to another, steadily spying as you go, you will probably find yourself more tired than if you had walked many miles at a regular pace.

Seeing a roe for the first time, either as a distant chestnut speck or, all too obvious, alarmed at close quarters, can be intensely exciting. Even if it is a buck, do not necessarily expect to be asked to shoot – promising males are left for the good of the stock, or the guide may know of unexpected hazards such as houses, domestic stock, camping sites or whatever, which make the shot unsafe. Use your binoculars to identify and study. Maybe it will be a doe with fawns – a charming sight as they quietly feed, or enjoy the warmth of the rising sun. Study them,

savour the moment, and you will be getting the best out of your stalking.

When a shot presents itself, use any support available such as a nearby tree or a fencepost to steady your aim. The ultimate ambition of the roe stalker is to select an unsuspecting animal which, for the good of its race, should be culled, and then to make a shot which will ensure the minimum suffering. The difficulty of the shot, the size of the trophy, should make no difference to the satisfaction of coming home with a buck which has been carefully, humanely and properly shot. No eggs and bacon or coffee ever tasted half so good as after a morning's stalking such as this. That is what makes the devotees of roe stalking return year after year to a sport which only a fellow-enthusiast can really appreciate.

If you have the offer of a day or two's roe stalking, the time is going to be very precious and, unless you are very lucky, the transaction is going to cost a certain amount of money. There are many uncertainties that may wreck your chances of success, but if you do your homework

Roebuck – lithe, beautiful and a worthy quarry

30

you can at least ensure that, if the weather is reasonable and the chance of a shot comes up, you have made the most of a golden opportunity.

Quite simply, this means in general that your clothes must be comfortable and unobtrusive and that you have a suitable rifle, equipped with a telescopic sight, with which you are as familiar as possible. At one end you should have a squashy hat to shade the giveaway white of the face, while at the other footwear in which you can walk without pain for some hours without making a lot of noise. The notes which follow may help fill in the background of roe and roe stalking, and increase your enjoyment of your first taste of a very rewarding sport.

BACKGROUND

The graceful roebuck, undoubtedly beautiful, is either a pest or an asset, depending on your point of view. He is detested by those who plant trees only to have them destroyed the following night, and especially by rose growers whose choicest buds are singled out, usually just before bursting forth into their full glory.

For most of the half million or so years that he has lived here, the roe has been regarded as scarcely higher than the rat in the sporting hierarchy. There is, however, a small band of devoted admirers who love the roe and who have campaigned for better treatment in the years when the shotgun and the snare were accepted methods of control.

Nowadays, roe stalking is a well-established sport, unusual not only in the appalling hours which its devotees are expected to follow, but for the fact that as a sport it is almost always dominated by three objectives: the control of damage to forest, farm and garden crops; the development of humane methods of control; and good management for the wellbeing of the deer themselves. Roe have few natural predators since we eliminated the wolf, the lynx and the bear, and they are outstanding in the present-day wildlife scene for an ability not only to survive, but to multiply almost too successfully, in a wide variety of habitats. Roe can be found from the Highlands of Scotland to suburbia.

DESCRIPTION

Roe are the smallest of British native deer species, standing about 63 cm at the shoulder, and weighing between 22 and 27 kg. Unlike the larger species such as red or fallow deer, roe are individualists, living in pairs or small groups all the year. They are very adaptable, being found in thick forest, moorland and even farmland with little more than hedgerows and copses for shelter. In the summer they are bright chestnut, the males having short antlers, usually about 20–25 cm long, with typically six points. The ears are large and mobile, the nose black and moist, while the eyes are prominent, with an expression which is both beautiful and intelligent. In winter, the coat thickens and darkens, and a patch of white develops on the posterior which, in moments of alarm, can be fanned out until it resembles a large puffball. Their food is principally the leaves and twigs of trees and bushes. Large amounts of grass and growing corn are taken if there is no alternative.

DISTRIBUTION

During the Middle Ages, roe deer became very scarce in England, retreating towards the remoter parts of Scotland. They were not highly regarded as beasts of the chase and were, therefore, fair game for all and sundry, without the horrific penalties which Robin Hood and others risked when they pursued more lordly quarry. During the last century this trend was reversed. Roe are now abundant throughout Scotland and are extending their range southwards from the Border Counties into Lancashire, Yorkshire and beyond.

Southern England is now well populated by roe, from the eastern part of Cornwall to west Kent and northwards to the line of the Thames; stragglers have been reported well to the north even of this area. The present widespread population in the south owes its origins to reintroductions. The first of these was at Milton Abbas in Dorset in 1800, followed later that century by others at Thetford on the Norfolk–Suffolk border and elsewhere. The origin of the deer liberated in Dorset is not certain, but contemporary references seem to indicate they came from France. The Thetford deer came from Württemberg in Germany, and this population still remains distinct and isolated. An element of the original native stock just might remain in the Sussex roe, owing to escapes from woodland inside the 13-mile wall at Petworth Park, where roe are said to have survived since the original enclosure, although these may also have been imported. There is a marked difference in antler type between Sussex and Dorset roe, but, as both communities have spread, the two types are now in contact on a line roughly from Southampton north to Newbury, where one may expect the appearance of bucks of an intermediate type or with a marked hybrid vigour.

Roe are found wherever suitable cover exists, and sometimes in large numbers. Their breeding rate is high, and they have adapted extremely successfully to life in the overpopulated surroundings of much of southern England. Ideal conditions are the hardwood and coppice areas, where there is alternate high and low cover and an abundance of brambles and other favourite foods. However, roe can also exist equally well in the big spruce forests of Scotland and northern England and on open heather moors. Even a small copse provides harbour for a pair of roe, providing that food and cover are available.

Most people think that roe feed by preference at dawn and dusk, but this is only the result of long years of harassment; when men are active the roe keep their heads down. For this reason, stalking has developed the tradition of maximum effort at first and last light, but roe are extremely intelligent animals, studying humanity far more intently than they are studied. In areas where roe have been stalked night and morning for any length of time, they are once again changing their habits, and many a stalker finds it difficult to explain why he sees so few after getting up in the wee small hours, yet they are commonplace to the tractor driver and the forester.

The management of roe in Britain is almost always linked with limiting forest damage. Populations are not kept artificially high as a concession to sport, and, almost ironically, this is one reason why Britain has an enviable reputation for the quality of roe, and particularly for unusually fine roe trophies. While we continue to take this attitude and limit the density to well within the capacity of the woods to support it, we are unlikely to lose that quality. But we must always remember that the careful stalker replaces the long-vanished predator who was not preoccupied with antler quality, but rather with filling his belly with the nearest available prey. We should not therefore become obsessed by the trophy-hunting syndrome. Overexploitation of the male, while it will have no effect on the reproductive capacity of the herd or reduce the overall damage which is suffered by the local forester, will inevitably have an effect on trophy quality. For this reason, although we all love to go out for a buck in the summer mornings and rejoice when something memorable comes along, the real work of management is in the difficult business of culling enough does to balance the population during the short winter days. Nevertheless, it is buck stalking in the summer which first hooks most of us. The only problem is to know how to start.

STALKING

Stalking the roe is true still-hunting – the stalker moving gently about the woods, choosing times and places where the roe are likely to be active. This means that he must be prepared to get up early (very early in the north, where the summer nights are short). Similarly, he must abandon any thought of dinner in the evening. He should be out again in the woods until it is too dark to distinguish one animal from another. Roe have very fine senses, their powers of scent and hearing being remarkably acute. The whole business becomes one of prowling; a very slow, silent progress through the woods, minutely searching every possible area for the patch of colour, the flick of movement, or the partial silhouette which, if you are lucky, will betray a watchful roe. You stick to the paths because it is pointless to blunder through the wilder areas, and, if paths do not exist, you choose a suitable place and sit there, motionless, regardless of time

Two roe well away from cover

or midges, until something appears. In these circumstances, or where the land is so flat that it is not safe to shoot from ground level, many stalkers now use high seats. These are elevated platforms, where one can sit in varying degrees of comfort with a good view of the surrounding greenery.

Most of the pleasure of a stalking outing comes through the use of a good pair of binoculars, not only to observe the deer more closely but all the other wild creatures which may come and go in the course of a morning's stalk. Stalking with binoculars only, or with the addition of a camera, is pure pleasure. Stalking with a rifle and no binoculars is not only boring but is likely to be dangerous. Binoculars allow you to study and identify an animal before deciding whether it is shootable or otherwise. Even more important, the background must be most carefully observed to make sure that the bullet, which might easily pass through the animal, will safely bury itself in the ground beyond. Nobody who goes out stalking should underestimate the responsibility that using a rifle imposes on them.

CLOTHING

Serious buck stalking starts on 1 May, when the weather may still be pretty cold – in fact, at any time the stalker must be equipped for cool, rainy weather, although he always hopes for something better. For a long, wet session on a high seat, some sort of waterproof is desirable, but otherwise all clothing must have a soft finish, and should, in addition, be either in camouflage pattern or a mixture of muted colours that blends in with the woodland. It is better to get wet than to wear a waterproof jacket which scrapes against every passing twig, alerting the deer. Waterproof trousers should be left at home. A tweed hat is unobtrusive, shielding the eyes from sun and the back of the neck from rain. They leak after a time, but can be waterproofed with one of the proprietary sprays or by the slow accumulation of midge oil and sweat over the years. Lightweight leather shoes with ridged rubber soles are ideal for dry conditions, but on many occasions, particularly in the morning, rubber boots will be needed. They should preferably be the light-

33

weight sort which lace up the leg, and not gumboots in which it is almost impossible to walk silently.

That unpleasant character, the tick, is present in many parts of the country. The adults are large and disgusting; the larvae are minute and may be quite difficult to discover, even after a tickling sensation betrays their presence. They all delight in burying their heads in human skin, from which they are quite difficult to dislodge. Surgical spirit or nail-varnish remover are probably among the best methods, and pulling them off definitely the worst because they usually leave their mouthparts in the skin which immediately start to fester. In tick areas, trousers are preferable to breeches and stockings because the latter collect ticks as the stalker walks through the damp grass.

Mosquitoes and flies can also be a pest, particularly in damp, warm weather in the summer, and a good deterrent should be carried. They are sometimes so bad in the north that stalkers may be forced to use netting veils when stalking in late summer.

Roe stalkers tend to carry a rucksack, large enough to contain the roe that they are after. A spare sweater can also be carried against the chills of late evening or the first hour of the morning before the sun warms up.

RIFLES AND EQUIPMENT

A rifle of less than 6 mm calibre may not be used in England or Wales, although the .222 and the .22/250 are, at present, allowed in Scotland. In general, calibres between .243 Winchester and 8 mm are recommended. It is much more important that you are familiar with your rifle and capable of using it accurately from all positions than to worry whether one particular cartridge is better than another within the legal limits. Shots at roe will not be taken at long range, and most at less than 100 m. They are small targets and demand accurate shooting. For this reason, the rifle must be carefully zeroed, and this task, or pleasure, is one for you yourself, because no two people can depend on shooting accurately with the same sight setting. The bullet should not

strike more than 3 cm high at 100 m for roe, because of the short ranges. Check the rifle immediately before leaving home for a stalking holiday so that time is not wasted rezeroing when you are asked to fire a test group on arrival. This is normally insisted upon before stalking can begin.

A good telescopic sight is essential for roe stalking, because you are usually working in poor light and with uncertain backgrounds. There are likely to be up to ten screws securing it to the rifle. All these should be checked periodically for tightness, particularly before a zeroing session, because any looseness or variation from shot to shot will be fatal. The scope should be fitted with an aiming device or graticule, which is easily visible in bad light. In poor light plain cross-hairs are not usually very effective. A good thick post, preferably flat-topped, or a combination of posts and cross-hairs is less likely to let you down. Magnification should not exceed ×4. A pair of protective caps for the lenses is a good idea because the rifle will be carried ready for use on your shoulder and not in a case or slip. A good, crisp, single-stage trigger pull is probably the most important element in a good stalking rifle. A heavy, dragging pull may be acceptable for deliberate prone shooting, but when a shot is offered standing, as is so often the case with roe, the rifle will be pulled off centre before the shot leaves the barrel. Fit a sling to the rifle, because your hands will be busy with binoculars, one trusts, long before you need to use the rifle. The sling should be made of nonslip material, and it should be attached to the rifle in such a way that it doesn't rattle.

FIREARMS CERTIFICATES

Before you can use a rifle, you have to have a firearms certificate from the police. This applies even if the rifle is on loan – you are not covered by the owner's certificate. Most police forces insist on knowing what you want to use the rifle for, and will probably demand written evidence from a landowner that you have permission to stalk and that the ground is suitable for the use of a rifle. A very awkward hen-and-egg situation thus exists as you obviously can't stalk without a rifle, but you can't get a rifle without first having some stalking! There is also the question of delay while the official wheels are set in motion. Although many firearms departments will try hard to shorten the process, they have a laid-down procedure involving correspondence and inquiries, which may mean that weeks or even months elapse between your application and the granting of a certificate.

The stages are: first, you must apply to the police for a certificate, giving details of the type of rifle, but not necessarily the serial number, which you would like to acquire. Also the number of cartridges you want to buy at any one time, the number you want to possess and the number that you think you may use over the three-year currency of the certificate. When it arrives, you may go to any gunmaker and shop around for the sort of rifle you want. When the purchase is made it will be recorded on your certificate. Each time that you purchase ammunition you will also have to produce your certificate, a note being made on it by the gunmaker of the number of rounds supplied. A new certificate at present costs £25, and renewal or variation £20.

Some police forces insist on imposing a condition to the firearms certificate restricting use to certain named areas of land. It is as well to list all the likely places where you are planning to stalk, always remembering that the police will write to the owners named. It is embarrassing if they have not yet given you permission! Another hen-and-egg which needs very careful and tactful handling.

While in a legal vein, one should perhaps point out that although there is a large wild population of deer in this country, someone, usually the landowner, always has the right to shoot them, so permission must always be obtained. There is no free shooting, as is the case in parts of the United States, for example. The penalties for entering land in pursuit of deer are now substantial, and the fact that you missed, or did not even get a shot, does not constitute a defence.

Binoculars are always important. They should be of high quality and low magnification – not more than ×8. Binoculars are usually labelled with two measurements, the first being magnification and the second the size of the object lens, for example 7 × 50. Large object lenses of 40 or 50 mm are likely to give better visibility in poor light, while low magnification reduces the effect of shake and makes them quick to use. Some modern binoculars are straight in the barrel, so-called 'roof prisms', while others have the familiar hump shape. Roof prisms are more expensive to manufacture and, therefore, price for price, conventional prismatic binoculars are better value. Excellent 7 × 50s, a very good size for roe stalking, can still be obtained for about £30. Binoculars should be fitted with a strap so they can be carried around the stalker's neck available for instant use. The eyepieces should be protected with caps or a flap of leather.

If you are out single-handed, you will need a frameless rucksack large enough to carry a buck. In any case, it is a convenient receptacle for various pieces of equipment which will not go in your pocket. These items will come in useful sooner or later, and should be packed in individual polythene bags to keep them dry: gloves, matches, string, insect repellent, toilet paper, map and compass. A knife should always be carried – this needs to be sharp rather than of any particular design, although folding knives must have a lock blade.

During the summer, many shots will be taken from a standing or, at best, a sitting position, because of the amount of cover. This needs practice before your stalking holiday. You should learn to take advantage of any tree or fencepost which may be near enough, so that you shoot with reasonable accuracy and speed. Many stalkers who are used to thick woodland use a stick. In the case of a right-handed shot, it must be carried in the left hand, with the rifle slung on the right shoulder, muzzle down. The stick should be nearly as long as the stalker himself is tall, and need not have a fork on the top. It can be a great help in steadying both the rifle and the binoculars, but to become proficient you need to practice.

From time to time, small-scale moves, with one beater and possibly a dog, are used, either to dislodge a difficult buck or, more frequently, in the winter to help the doe cull along when numbers are almost always difficult to get. For this, one or two rifles, at most three, ambush the deer in places where the deer will stop to look back and where they can be safely shot. This allows them to be identified and the correct ones shot. Large-scale drives are not acceptable, and, with the sole exception of a wounded animal likely to escape, no deer should be shot while running.

CALLING

The roe rut, or breeding season, which starts in mid-July and goes on to mid-August, is an exciting time to be out in the woods. One is conscious of a new spirit of excitement among the roe after the dog days of late June and early July when they keep fairly quiet. Hopeful bucks can be seen questing, nose to ground, and unaccompanied does will attract them, not only by scent, but in a language of shrill squeaks which can be imitated, sometimes with exciting results!

Courting among roe, particularly when the weather is hot and fine, takes the form of prolonged chases, during which the buck makes a throaty panting noise – once heard, not easily forgotten. Roe are not monogamous, and one doe may accept the favours of several bucks sometimes in the course of a few hours. Using a call to attract bucks is an art, and some stalkers are very skilled at it, though, on the whole, this technique is not as widely practised in Britain as in Europe. If we are lucky enough to have hot, thundery weather at the peak of the rut, then calling can be extremely exciting. It is usually most effective between 9 a.m. and 2 p.m. August is, however, a period when the weather is frequently wet and windy and, under these conditions, calling is usually ineffective. For this reason a stalking holiday at this time of year can be memorable, or a complete disaster.

A variety of roe calls can be purchased, but it is generally reckoned that success depends more on where and when one calls than on the particular cadences used, though these are undoubtedly important. One can squeak like a distressed fawn, hoping that the doe will emerge, to be closely followed by a buck. Alternatively, a lower, peeping noise imitates the cry of a doe in season, while louder, squealing noises are assumed to represent the slightly alarmed cry of a young doe when closely pressed by a buck. This last can produce explosive results because any buck within earshot knows that he has to be quick!

The art of calling cannot be learned from a book; one hour with an expert is worth many pages of print.

GETTING STARTED

Unless you are exceptionally lucky, your first chance to go roe stalking is not going to be easy to find and is likely to be quite expensive. Even if you know someone who has deer on his land, he cannot be expected to leap at the suggestion that you should stalk them, as stalking these days has a definite commercial value. Even if the owner is more concerned about protecting his crops from damage than making money out of the deer, he may be hesitant to give a beginner armed with a lethal weapon free range over his land. In other cases, particularly where there is a valuable pheasant shoot, neither owner nor keeper may wish to have any disturbance in the woods at a time when the birds are nesting. The keeper may be too busy to cope with visitors at this time of year. But the first chunk of stalking experience, though expensive, may eventually prove the gateway to better, cheaper opportunities in the future.

So, you are consumed with interest in deer, and filled with an insatiable desire to get a set of antlers, however modest, to hang on the wall. How do you go about it? The first thing, of course, is to find out as much as you can, and these days there are quite a few sources of information through books (a short list of titles is included on page 39) and by contacting fellow-enthusiasts. This latter can be most easily achieved by joining the British Deer Society. This organization has branches all over the country which not only organize social and informative meets, usually at places where there

End of a roe stalk. Jack takes aim

are deer, but also arrange training courses and tests, so that the would-be stalker can prove to himself, if to nobody else, that he has done his basic homework.

If you really can't afford to pay for your fun, then the only thing to do is make yourself useful. For those who are fortunate enough to live in deer country, this may take the form of helping a stalker put up high seats and perhaps, eventually, assist in the doe cull. Those less well placed can make themselves so indispensable at society events that, sooner or later, someone is going to

37

Jack and Richard Prior with a young buck displaying a poor-quality head

respond to real keenness and offer some sort of stalking opportunity, no matter how problematical. From these small beginnings, much can develop.

Otherwise, you have to buy yourself in. The easiest way of doing that is through hotel stalking. Many hotels, particularly in the north, advertise the fact that they have stalking available; in addition to the hotel bill and the costs of getting there, you can expect to pay for your stalking pleasure. The well-lined will, of course, go for a buck, probably accompanied by a professional stalker or keeper who will make the decision about what to shoot in accordance with the rules of good management. Obviously the overheads for this type of red-carpet sport are high, and each mature buck shot carries a considerable charge, not only in terms of time

spent taking the client out and locating him, but in shooting the does and young bucks which form the larger part of the cull each year. In round terms this type of sport is quite likely to cost £100 or more per buck and, should you happen to shoot a large trophy, could be considerably more. Anyone who can't afford a lot of money but still desperately wants to get into the stalking world should explain his dilemma to the hotel proprietor or to the sporting agent, saying that he would love to go out stalking but would be quite happy to take young bucks or to make a date for the winter to help the keeper with the does. The cost is likely to be considerably less, and the experience just as valuable.

No matter what style of stalking you go for, it is much better to go the whole hog and have a week at it, not just a day or two. Roe stalking is

38

among the most uncertain of sports, and luck and weather play a big part. Fog, rain, high winds, cold and half a dozen other elements can wreck the prospects, sometimes for several days. If you have only a couple of days to spare and things go wrong, the whole venture can be something of a fiasco. If, on the other hand, success comes early, all you have as a souvenir is a pair of knobbly bones and a large bill. Stalking memories should be of the glories of the forest, the song of birds in the morning just as the sun rises, the companionship of your stalker, who is sure to be a fellow-enthusiast. These things are not acquired in the course of a few short hours or in the hectic neck-or-nothing pursuit of a trophy as the one object of the whole excursion.

Many agents, hotels and individual estates offer a package deal of a week's stalking which will entitle you to a specified number of bucks, some of which may be yearlings at a nominal fee, while the mature trophy bucks will carry fees commensurate with their size, in addition to the price you pay for a week of accompanied stalking. A glance at the advertisements in the *Shooting Times* will suggest several addresses. It is always worth asking for the names of previous clients so that you can find out from them what sort of sport they enjoyed, and whether it fits in with the type of holiday you have in mind. The standards of game management and of service to the visitor, besides the price, may vary widely between one estate and another.

TROPHIES

The typical roe head has six points, and is about 24 cm in length. Every year a number of exceptional trophies are taken (often by complete beginners) and the fortunate stalker often wonders how his trophy compares with national or international standards. Ideally, the antlers must be rough or, as the term goes, well-pearled, with well-marked coronets, the wider bands round the base of the antler. The points should be long, and the two antlers roughly symmetrical. The record for length is over 33 cm, but anything over 25 cm is good, though this is not the only point which is taken into consideration when assessing a trophy against an accepted standard. International trophy shows are held in one country or another about every ten years, at which great care is taken to arrive by means of a formula at an official score for each trophy shown, so that the owners can make a direct comparison between one and another. If this results in an unhealthy spirit of competition, it is to be regretted. Setting this aside, it is interesting to know whether your favourite trophy measures up to the sort of standard which would give it a place of honour in an international gathering. Britain has a very high reputation for big roe trophies.

To get an unofficial score, according to the international rules, it is only necessary to send your trophy to the Game Conservancy at Fordingbridge, which will, for a modest fee, measure the head and issue a certificate showing the estimated score according to the international formula. They also issue gold, silver and bronze commemorative medals for trophies reaching the agreed standards, a continental tradition which has recently taken firm root in this country. Details of this service may be obtained by application to the Game Conservancy, Fordingbridge, Hampshire.

FURTHER READING

British Deer Society, *Field Guide to British Deer* (Blackwell)

The Forestry Commission, *The Roe Deer* (HMSO)

Frank Holmes, *Following the Roe* (Bartholomew)

Herbert Krebs, *Young or Old?* (S.C. Mayer)

Richard Prior, *Roe Deer: Management and Stalking* (Game Conservancy)

Richard Prior, *The Roe Deer of Cranborne Chase* (Oxford)

Henry Tegner, *The Roe Deer* (Tideline)

INFORMATION ON DEER

The British Deer Society
The Mill House
Bishopstrow
Warminster
Wilts.

Ian Coghill with some of his minkhounds

MINKHUNTING

Ian Coghill

Minkhunting is not a sport in the sense that coarse fishing or pheasant shooting are sports. The overriding essential in minkhunting is to catch as many mink as possible. The constraints of achieving this are imposed by humaneness and not by sportsmanship.

Minkhunting can be enjoyable and is always interesting, but the sporting element, the sporting chance that the mink has of escaping, is dictated by the mink, the terrain in which it is hunted and the natural and inevitable limitations of the hounds and men that pursue it.

There is no conscious effort to allow the mink a sporting chance by stopping hounds or giving it a start, or law as it is called, as the farming community, water bailiffs and gamekeepers, by whose respective invitation and permission we hunt, would not tolerate such behaviour.

The mink is unquestionably the most unpopular of the predatory animals currently found in the British Isles. In spite of some rather obvious efforts to whitewash the mink's reputation by people who would abolish traditional country sports, those who are subject to its depredations are in no doubt as to its destructive potential. The mink is not a natural inhabitant of our rivers and streams and, as a result, many of our indigenous wildlife species, including fish, birds and mammals valued as game, and also others whose continued survival as breeding species is already at risk, have developed no natural defences against their attacks.

In addition, mink are amazingly powerful for their size and as they can climb like squirrels, swim like otters, run as fast as rabbits and go through the smallest of holes, they pose an ever-present hazard to the keepers of poultry, waterfowl and to many types of pets.

When mink first began escaping from fur farms they aroused little concern as their extremely violent courtship behaviour made them difficult and uncertain breeders in unnatural conditions. These early escapes were considered merely as interesting, but definitely local, problems which would soon burn themselves out. Too late it was recognized that the wild mink bred with amazing efficiency, and the Ministry of Agriculture began a campaign of eradication. This was, as usual, too little too late, and the mink continued to increase and spread steadily. Eventually the Ministry was forced to give up its costly and, as it proved, pointless efforts and admit that eradication was impossible.

It was by then clear that overall control and some local eradication were the best that could be achieved and even these efforts were entirely dependent on private efforts.

Keepers and some water bailiffs had always trapped as many mink as they could, but this was, and is, a time-consuming and unpleasant business. Some farmers and conservationists also took direct action when the need and opportunity arose but such efforts were inevitably spasmodic and local and they left many areas where, for a variety of reasons, no control operated. What was clearly needed was a form of control that followed the mink into its previously undisturbed strongholds, but operated on an area basis, able to cross farm and estate boundaries and deal with the problem in a logical way.

A properly organized minkhunt provides just such a service. The one with which I am involved hunts by invitation and permission over more than 1000 separate farms and estates and thus is able to fill in the gaps left by other control techniques.

Our ability to function effectively over such a wide area depends entirely on the support and goodwill of the farming community. There exists a no more hospitable group of people in Great Britain, but their hospitality, rich and bottomless as it is, in turn depends on very definite but usually unstated rules. One of these is that whilst they are entirely happy that the hunters who cross their land in pursuit of mink should enjoy themselves, they expect them to do as efficient a job as possible in dealing with the mink.

Anyone who is inefficient or merely out to fool about will soon be told not to bother to come again. Thus the organizers of a minkhunt are expected to be good at their job and, from the point of view of the rural community, that job is very clearly understood to be the business of catching mink.

Mink are small, fast and agile. A 4-lb mink would be exceptionally large and many are only 1–2 lb in weight. Their scent, which hounds must follow, is very variable and as they can swim under water, go into narrow holes, climb trees and thread the densest cover, they present hounds and hunters with a formidable challenge.

One of the principal pleasures in minkhunting, for me at least, lies in overcoming this challenge. The breeding, training and handling of a small pack of hounds which, in spite of the many difficulties, regularly catch their quarry is something I find fascinating.

To this pleasure I would add the enormous satisfaction that comes from successfully liaising with countless farmers, keepers, landowners, fishermen and others, men and women who include many who are the salt of the earth. The final ingredient for me is provided by the joy of having permission to walk the banks of some of Britain's most beautiful rivers and streams during every season of the year and in every weather.

Abolitionists will no doubt claim that I have omitted to mention the pleasure I get from killing, but I have omitted nothing. We enjoy hunting, not killing. As we are engaged in a serious attempt at pest control it is, of course, obvious that our hunting involves killing our quarry, but to say that we enjoy it or to pretend that the kill is a major incentive to any hunter is no more realistic than to claim that people who enjoy a well-cooked sirloin enjoy killing cattle.

There is no such thing as an average mink-hunting establishment. Each hunt reflects the ideas and personalities of the men and women in control. Each must respond to its own local circumstances. There are, however, certain characteristics which are common to most.

Each hunt will have one Master or two or more Joint Masters, a picturesque if somewhat archaic title whose meaning would be better expressed in modern English by the term manager. It is their job to run the hunt on behalf of the committee who appointed them; to arrange kennelling; plan the season's hunting; breed and produce hounds; liaise with landowners and farmers; and generally take responsibility for everything that facilitates the successful running of the hunt. To this end they will be assisted, like the managers of any other club, by an honorary treasurer and honorary secretary and by such hunt staff as they choose to appoint.

The hunt staff, who may be amateur or professional, will include a huntsman, one or more whippers-in and a terrierman. Each job has its own specific skills and also involves skills which are common to the other roles.

Contrary to popular belief, each group of hunters accompanying a pack of hounds in the hunting field contains only one huntsman; he is the man who is said to be 'carrying the horn', which is an apt expression as no one else is allowed to carry or use the short copper and nickel English hunting horn as an aid to manoeuvring the pack and its attendant helpers and followers. The huntsman is responsible for the tactics of the day: he will decide where hounds will draw, or search for a mink; he will dictate the pace and thoroughness of the draw; when hounds lose a scent he must use his experience and innate skill to help them refind it. It is he who will decide when a mink is finally lost and that further searching is useless, and when hounds should be encouraged or restrained. In short, the success of any given day or the long-term success of the hunt as a whole is largely dependent on the skill of the huntsman.

A wise old hound

His principal assistants are the whippers-in, whose relationship with the huntsman is similar to that which exists in a football match between the linesmen and their referee. The whippers-in are the huntsman's long-distance eyes and ears and can either report back or take action themselves. The name whipper-in is an archaic and honorary title and certainly should not be taken to imply that its bearers are constantly using their whips. No well-bred hound properly handled needs beating. A whipper-in is expected to be able to control the pack and its individual members in the same manner as the huntsman, by using his voice and eye.

The final member of hunt staff, the terrier-man, keeps and handles the terriers which accompany the hounds and which are called into use when the mink goes to ground.

The final human ingredient of any minkhunt is the field, the traditional term for the people who follow the hunt. Everyone involved in hunting, whatever their present rank or title, has at some time been a member of the field and it is from the ranks of the followers that new generations of hunt staff are recruited. In addition, it is the daily 'cap' money and subscriptions paid by people who want to accompany the hunt that pay most of the bills, so in many ways the field is an important ingredient of the hunt.

No one who is prepared to behave properly is barred from following the hunt. The only proviso is that he or she must in no way abuse the hospitality of our farmer hosts and must not interfere with the efficient handling of the hounds. It should be remembered, however, by anyone wishing to hunt that many farmers put limits on the number of people, no matter how well behaved they are, that they are prepared to welcome on their land. A man who might welcome twenty or even fifty people along his brook might view the passage of 200 or 300 in a different light. Minkhunting continues through the height of the spring and summer growing season, when stock is in the fields and when crops of hay and corn are vulnerable to damage. Intending followers should therefore expect to be subjected to pretty strict control as to where they may walk and what they may do under such circumstances.

Newcomers are always welcome but they should realize that from the hunt's point of view they present a risk, as one thoughtless act can injure vital relationships that have been built up over many years of trust and responsible behaviour. Furthermore, a Master already concerned about the large size of his following may not be entirely overjoyed by the idea of increasing it still further.

Intending followers can help to make their reception easier by demonstrating to the Master or secretary their responsible attitude to the countryside and its traditions. It is easiest for those who are already known to be responsible members of hunts which operate in the winter months, such as packs of beagles and foxhounds, and it is helped immeasurably by the knowledge that the would-be follower is a fully paid up member of the British Field Sports Society.

Anyone wishing to hunt can find the address of the secretary of his local hunt by writing to the secretary of the Masters of Minkhounds Association or in some cases by studying the relevant section in *Baily's Hunting Directory* or in the *Annual Directory of Hunts* published by *Horse and Hound*. Never be shy about asking permission to hunt, as once you have shown your intention to act responsibly you will find no warmer or more entertaining crowd than the men and women who follow hounds.

The cost of minkhunting is minimal; indeed, if you are a farmer or farm worker it will cost you nothing as, in common with keepers and other hunt benefactors, you will normally be entitled to hunt free of charge, although naturally many like to make a donation in one form or another. My own hunt has an annual subscription of £20 and a day's cap of £1 for people who do not subscribe. Other costs, apart from getting to the meet, are nonexistent, as special clothing is not necessary. Any clothes, preferably not new, suitable for a long country walk will suffice for minkhunting.

A few tips to bear in mind are that most people find wellington boots extremely uncomfortable after a mile or so; that you are likely to get both wet and dirty; and that a change of clothing is handy if not actually essential at the end of the day. In hot weather a hat can prevent sunburn, and those not carrying a serviceable walking stick have only themselves to blame if they get a ducking.

Most minkhunts meet every Saturday from April to the end of September and many will also aim to arrange an additional weekly mid-week meet. Some hunts will turn out more often, especially during July and August when complaints of mink damage seem to reach an annual peak. Several hunts also arrange joint weeks when two packs will hunt alternate days in a given area, thus hunting every day of the week. Such a strategy has proved particularly effective in my own hunt's territory, enabling us to catch in a single week twice as many mink as the Ministry of Agriculture trappers caught in the same area in their last twelve months of operation.

All Saturday and many mid-week meets will be at 11 a.m. but many hunts arrange evening meets at 5 or 6 p.m. during the working week, thus enabling the hunt staff to get their work done and yet still allow the hunt to keep up with requests for assistance from mink-pestered farmers and keepers.

When a newcomer arrives at a meet he should introduce himself to the honorary secretary and the Master and pay his cap. He should also make certain that his transport is not parked so as to cause embarrassment to local people or to other road users, and remember that everything that goes down a country lane is not an ordinary car; combine harvesters are extremely wide and they and other farm machinery have an absolute right of passage.

When the hunt moves off all he is expected to do is to walk along with the other followers and watch what goes on. A beginner's interest and enjoyment will be considerably enhanced if he asks the Master or secretary to introduce him to a regular who can act as guide and interpreter. Do not be put off if during the day the Master and his hunt staff are disinclined to explain the finer points of the chase. Remember that they have their respective jobs to do and much depends on the degree of concentration they can maintain; they will have little time left for conversation.

There is no such thing as a typical day but the beginner can expect to see several key phases during his first few days' hunting. The huntsman will take hounds to the water and they will begin to draw, normally upstream. The whippers-in will walk in front, one on each bank, looking for signs of mink activity such as tracks, droppings and freshly killed prey, and will gently check any hounds inclined to draw more quickly than the rest. The hounds will be on both banks with some questing along the water line and examining likely nooks and crannies for the scent of the mink.

The huntsman will walk quietly behind the pack watching them for any indication of interest, subtly adjusting the pace of the pack to accord with the terrain they have to deal with, and sending them across to likely places they may have missed. Whilst this phase of a day's hunting could be said by some people to be merely blank it will provide much interest for the discerning

The field comes from all walks of life

follower. It is akin to the dour and runless yet skilled early survival of an opening batsman on a bad wicket. To someone who knows how easy it is to make a mistake it has its own fascination.

When hounds pick up the overnight scent of a mink they are said to be 'hunting the drag'. At first the hounds will begin to draw more keenly, leaving the bank in increasing numbers and swimming up against the current, 'winding' or sniffing the water margin for the thin ghosts of scent left by the hunting mink several hours before. As the scent gets stronger the deepest scenting hounds (those with the best noses) will start to speak. This is neither a bark nor a howl nor even a bay, all of which are in a hound's vocabulary, but a quite distinct and musical note unique to each hound and produced only when the hounds are hunting the scent of their true quarry. Soon, if all goes well, the whole pack will be hunting the drag, racing upstream, plunging

through the shallows, swimming the pools. With every hound intent on following and enjoying the drag it is all too easy to overshoot the mink itself. This is especially the case when there are several mink about as individual drags will overlap in the most confusing way.

The beginner may therefore be surprised to see the hounds stopped and taken back to draw a piece of cover that they have just passed, but frequently this is the result of the huntsman seeing some slight indication from his best hounds that such a tactic might meet with their approval and it often proves to be successful.

The drag is a fascinating phase of the hunt: it is musical, exciting, full of expectation and suspense, and it provides a rare insight into what the mink has been doing during the hours of darkness.

The mink may actually be found in a variety of ways. The drag may merge imperceptibly with

45

the fresh line of the mink as it moves away from the approaching hounds, or the hounds may suddenly stop, realizing they have come to the end of the drag, and race back to the fresh scent of the mink which is now doubling back behind them. In both cases the mink is said to have been found 'lying rough', in other words merely sleeping above ground in some thick cover such as brambles or reeds.

Often, however, the mink is lying up in a hole or hollow tree, in which case hounds will 'mark', which they do by digging at the hole, baying into it and refusing point blank to consider leaving it unless ordered to do so. If the mink doesn't leave of its own accord, the terriers, accompanied by some judicious digging, will normally result in it 'bolting'.

However the mink has been found, the hunt proper now begins. The mink rarely bothers to go very far and prefers to use its agility, small size and swimming prowess to baffle the hounds. The scent of the mink is relatively faint and the more it doubles and twists about, the more the banks and water become 'foiled' with the scent of its pursuers and the harder it becomes for them to follow. Thus, ironically, the longer a minkhunt goes on, the greater become the mink's chances of escape. Most successful hunts are very short and most long hunts end in the mink's favour – exactly the opposite to what the layman might expect.

About half the mink that escape are simply lost by hounds which, for a variety of reasons, are no longer able to locate and follow the mink's scent.

Minkhunting takes you into the heart of the countryside

Most of the rest which evade capture do so by getting to ground. During the hunt mink may harbour in a wide variety of holes and, where possible, the terrier and, if necessary, a spade are used to bolt them; but as mink can get into difficult and extremely small places any hole may mean a sudden end to the pursuit of that particular mink. In areas where field drains are numerous, they present a serious problem as almost all will have a riverside opening and, being narrow and deep, they are more or less impregnable.

Unlike other quarry hunted by hounds in the United Kingdom, mink frequently go up trees. It is truly remarkable how swiftly some hounds master the knack, hunting the mink's scent on the bark of trees and announcing to the world that their quarry is now hidden in an ivy-covered trunk 20 feet above their heads. When this happens, hounds will be taken away and one of the followers will be dispatched to climb the tree and drive the mink down again. If this proves impossible or if the farmer requests it, a gun will normally be sent for and the mink shot.

If the mink is not lost, shot or gone safely to ground, hounds will eventually catch it. Hounds kill naturally; they do not start their hunting careers until they are twelve or eighteen months old, and by that time their instinctive ability to kill small prey swiftly and surely is fully developed. Hounds are not taught to kill their quarry any more than cats are taught to catch mice.

The hounds used to hunt mink normally weigh 60–80 or even 100 lb, up to sixty times the bodyweight of their quarry. They are muscular creatures; to hunt at all effectively they must be in superb physical condition. Nothing can kill a mink quicker than such a hound.

Many people who are less concerned with humaneness than with the look of the thing make a great deal of fuss about hounds eating their quarry, or 'tearing it to pieces' as they prefer to put it. Hunting people take a different view. We believe that what matters is the swiftness of the kill and that animals, be they mink or bacon pigs, do not suffer *after* they are killed. What matters is not the look of the thing but its swiftness.

A mink caught in a trap for hours on end and finally drowned, which is the normal end for a trapped mink, will look, in spite of its suffering, as though it died in its sleep. A mink killed by hounds will die instantly but conversely its appearance may give great offence to people who would be unmoved by the sight of its trapped relative.

This brings us to the last but, for me, the most important facet of minkhunting, the hounds themselves. Hounds are for me the finest of creatures and I will make no apology for discussing them at some length; if talking about hounds is not to your taste it is probable that minkhunting, which is arguably the most hound-oriented of country sports, will not be either.

The British breed the best horses and the best hounds in the world and none of our established hound breeds is intrinsically unsuited to minkhunting or incapable of contributing something. In my own hunt we have tried every available breed and most crosses and whilst some were better than others none was without use.

Beagles and bassets have, when given the chance, entered to the scent of the mink and will hunt it as well as can be expected for a hound bred to follow the delicate scent of the hare. Bassets are certainly much more agile than might be imagined by those who have only seen them in advertisements. Even so, the type of terrain favoured by the mink is extremely unsuitable for a dog like the basset to manoeuvre in. This handicap has one advantageous spin-off in that the basset is often more inclined to swim than some of its more athletic friends; for such short legs the water provides a more comfortable option than the briar-infested bank.

Beagles are very agile and their small size enables them to make excellent progress through dense cover, but this does have some disadvantages. When hunting in the same pack as larger breeds, the ability of one or two beagles to wriggle quickly through cover is a positive disadvantage as they foil or destroy the scent before the other hounds can force their way along the same line. The pack soon gets disgusted with the situation and hounds will quickly start to abandon the unequal struggle and start to cut corners, with potentially disastrous consequences to the cohesion and effectiveness of the pack. Another problem with beagles is their small size, which makes them very vulnerable to the chilling effects of cold water. They are unlikely to enjoy a day that involves much water work.

Harriers, both the so-called stud book and the West Country types, can be very good, being quick, intelligent and positively eager to do what they are told. We have had some excellent examples of both breeds, with some absolutely outstanding West Country harriers. These were lovely white bitches, delightful characters, as sharp as needles with fine voices and an extraordinary ability to climb trees that suggested a monkey outcross some way back in their pedigrees.

Fell hounds are magnificent foxhunters, lithe and exceptionally athletic, but they are birds of their own country, dearly loved by the men who breed them and rarely parted with. They are possessed of a longevity that borders on immortality and seem able to contribute to the hunting of foxes at an age when other breeds would have lost their pace. As a result fell hounds have rarely appeared in a minkhunter's hound list. We have had only one, which proved excellent, being tough, a brilliant catcher of mink and intelligent enough to be a better conversationalist than some of our followers.

Dumfriesshire foxhounds are another numerically small but useful breed. These hounds, to the layman probably the most arresting of all breeds to look upon, were literally created by one man, Sir John Buchanan-Jardine. By blending the blood of French staghounds, bloodhounds and English foxhounds and then carefully selecting for the qualities he desired, he produced in an amazingly short space of time his own unique breed. What he had created were large hounds, at least by British standards, with the doghounds reaching up to 28 inches at the shoulder, beautiful to look at, with a bloodhound's nose and a voice to turn a human's blood to ice, and all wrapped up in a coat of purest black. Individually they are striking, as a pack they look magnificent, in full cry they can be downright awe-inspiring.

The present master of the Dumfriesshire Foxhounds, Sir Rupert Buchanan-Jardine, has maintained the pack to his father's exacting standards and has been more than generous in providing draft hounds for other packs, including some which hunt mink. There is no doubt that good specimens of this breed are potentially amongst the best minkhounds available and all are worth the most searching trial.

The pure otterhound is now sadly very rare, but the breed's best characteristics are being preserved in several packs of minkhounds, principally by carefully crossing the old breed with others such as the Welsh foxhound, which it resembles physically to a considerable extent.

The old breed had its problems and its detractors: by foxhound standards they have rather funny feet; their long ears, bloodhound heads and long curly coats do not suit everyone; and it must be admitted that some are inclined to think that they have done enough after a couple of hours of hard hunting, but when they are good, they are very, very good. The best are exceptional hounds to draw, patient and painstaking, the finest hounds to hunt a drag and fierce and accurate markers. They are equipped with the best of noses and glorious voices and make first-rate minkhounds.

Unfortunately there are now so few pure-bred otterhounds that the breed can barely hold its own, so many packs are forced to crossbreed in an attempt to acquire a degree of hybrid vigour to reduce the inevitable wastage that further inbreeding would cause.

This is a technique which I have used successfully myself. I aim to have between third and half my pack bred along this line, crossing Welsh hounds, principally from David Davies stock, with otterhounds descended from the Dumfriesshire and Border Counties. So far, results have been excellent, providing hounds that excel on the drag but which are tough and accurate enough to make a major contribution in the hunt proper.

Pure Welsh foxhounds are delightful creatures: small, wiry and rough coated, they are like the men who breed them, both independent and musical. Staunch and as true as steel, of all the

Mink are semi-aquatic and hounds must spend much of their time in the water

hound breeds the Welsh foxhound is the animal that suffers fools least gladly. They will do anything for a man they respect but if you are incompetent enough to lose their confidence they have an ability for selective and contemptuous deafness that has to be seen to be believed.

I have been lucky enough to be at the receiving end of a great deal of Welsh generosity and the Three Counties Minkhounds have as a result always had a few Welsh hounds, virtually all of which have made first-rate minkhunters. As a breed they are great finders and exceptional markers and can add a great deal to the overall efficiency of any pack of minkhounds.

Last but in no sense least is the dear old English foxhound. No finer creature exists. They have greater stamina than any beast that walks on earth; apparently impervious to cold, wet and discomfort, they are brave, intelligent, honest and biddable (in lay terms obedient).

The English foxhound rarely makes much noise on the drag and many will only speak on the fresh scent, but they are always in the vanguard, their indefatigable energy and drive making them unhappy unless they are at the head. They are at their best during long, hard days, when mink are apparently in every bush and when the hunting is fast and furious, flinging themselves into their work, never tiring, never questioning the need to press on, over, round or through any obstacle that stands between them and their quarry. Properly handled they will turn as their quarry turns like a stoat with a rabbit. As a breed they are the least likely to 'dwell' or linger on the scent of the mink and are often the first to say that he has slipped away unseen by even the sharpest human eyes.

Foxhounds are the backbone of my own hunt; I am never happy unless they make up at least half the pack. No hound is more pleasant to

49

End of the day – blowing for home

handle, they are as relaxed as only the brave can be, yet they are sharper than needles and their dry sense of humour ensures that every moment in their company is both a lesson and a joy.

By way of a summary I should say that minkhunting fulfils a useful function. It takes place in the real and imperfect world where controlling wild pests is neither easy nor an exact science. It is as humane as any pest-control operation can be expected to be and it is the only method of mink control subject to any code of conduct whatsoever.

For anyone who is interested in working dogs, especially working scent hounds, and who does not mind strenuous exercise and getting wet, minkhunting is full of interest.

The sight of hounds drawing difficult cover or galloping full cry through a rock-strewn gorge, the sound of them marking their quarry to ground in a tangle of roots, all these are things that no hound or working-dog lover will forget. With minkhunting these sights and innumerable others equally memorable can be savoured in the knowledge that at the same time one is helping to control an unwanted and alien pest with the fullest support of the rural community.

The mink is a worthy and difficult quarry when treated with the respect that all wild creatures deserve, and its pursuit has unquestionably enriched my own life and that of many of my friends. There are hounds and people I have come to know whom I shall never forget.

I have never asked anyone to go hunting. All I have ever asked is that before anyone gives an opinion about me and what I do he or she should see at first hand what goes on. For those who want to do so, I can guarantee that they will be welcome, but they should be warned that when they least expect it they may find that they are enjoying themselves.

High and overhead – the classic shot on a driven day

PHEASANT SHOOTING

John Ransford

In the last twenty years the pheasant has undoubtedly become the most widely distributed game bird in the British Isles. This is largely due to the work of the Game Conservancy, based at Fordingbridge, Hampshire, which has produced and perfected mechanical methods for hand-rearing and releasing the poults.

The pheasant is not indigenous to this country; it was introduced to Europe from Asia, possibly by the Romans, and has been very successful. It has thrived as a wild bird in the drier, warmer counties of the south and east; in the north and west, however, it would probably not have survived without artificial rearing.

As land usage has gradually altered over the years, with emphasis on growing cereals and less unhoused stock, the pheasant's natural year-round feed has changed. And, with the disappearance of thousands of miles of hedgerows, the draining of vast acreages, and the growth of large-scale monoculture farming, the pheasant's natural habitat has largely been destroyed.

Before the last war and until the mid-fifties, hedgerow berries were the pheasant's staple food from November until March. From April to October the mixed cropping of former years produced the cereals – which were almost entirely spring sown – that fed the stock birds in April, May and June. June, the month when most young pheasants hatched, was also the time when insect life was at its most abundant, and the young chicks had protein in profusion. In the

autumn the corn was cut by binder and the stooks left to stand out in the fields for several weeks; the heads that were shed as the sheaves were loaded on the wagon produced all the food the wild birds needed. Ploughing did not begin until October and the birds were able to forage quite late into the winter.

The farming pattern has changed in the past twenty-five years, with most cereal crops being sown in the autumn. Modern drills are so efficient at burying the seed that there is no spillage for the birds. Pesticides and herbicides have reduced the insect life at hatching time. Consequently hand-rearing of pheasants has become so widespread that there are very few estates that rely solely on wild birds.

In eastern and southern counties before the war, hand-rearing was rarely necessary and huge bags of wild pheasants were shot annually. The gamekeeper's job was ruthlessly to kill all predators and ground vermin that were likely to interrupt the production of wild pheasants; he only artificially fed his stock in the lean months of the year. In the colder, wetter areas of the northwest, hand-rearing of pheasants was in full swing and very large numbers were produced before the war. The rearing was done on large well-keepered estates and only the strays reached the smallholders' few acres. Pheasant shooting was, therefore, only undertaken by the wealthy and the privileged. Today, with many of the large estates broken up, there are far more

53

privately owned smaller areas, and hand-rearing is so easy that small farmers are producing a few pheasants each year, thus enabling many more people to partake in the sport of pheasant shooting.

In the 1920s and 1930s there was great rivalry between the estate owners as to who could shoot the most birds in a day, with bags of up to 2000 birds being common. These days, with cash less readily available, sportsmen prefer to shoot fewer birds over more days and the emphasis is on quality rather than quantity.

On the flat lands it is difficult to produce the high pheasants similar to those one sees driven across the steep valleys of the Welsh and Scottish borders. In Lincolnshire or Cambridgeshire the shoot manager or owner has to be inventive when driving pheasants; he has to place his Guns a sufficient distance from the covert crops to allow the birds to rise and cross the gun line at the optimum height, whereas in undulating country-side it is easy to flush the birds from hill top woodlands and stand the Guns on the floor of the valley.

Many of our woodland areas and shelter belts, which are now very important as amenities, were originally planted as pheasant coverts; on many estates there are famous drives, from both small and large woodlands, that were planted especially for pheasant shooting.

The pheasant keeper has a very busy life: a successful pheasant season begins in February, although the shooting does not start until October. The success of the shooting season depends on the keeper's efforts in the spring and summer. His first job, after the season has ended, is to catch enough stock to produce the poults for the following year. He has to catch a ratio of seven hens to one cock. These are placed either in small pens, each containing one cock and his hens, or in large wire enclosures where as many as 250 hens plus the correct proportion of cocks are kept. These days the breeding stock is fed on a balanced ration in a pellet form, but in the early days, hard corn was fed. On some game farms, the hens lay as many as fifty eggs per bird, whereas before the war, twenty per bird was considered good.

Until comparatively recently, all the eggs were incubated by broody hens. The broodies were placed in long lines of nestboxes and the first job for the keeper each morning was to lift them from their boxes, tether them by the leg and feed and water them; each bird was given about fifteen minutes out of her box. This continued for the twenty-four days that it takes pheasant eggs to hatch.

The success rate using modern incubators is not as high as using broodies; 65 per cent is considered average these days, whereas the broody hen often produced 90 per cent. Many of the older school of keepers still prefer to use broody hens but, sadly, the right type of broody is no longer available. Whereas the broody hen produced the warmth required for the young chicks, protected them from danger and taught them how to survive, we now use mechanical methods, with gas, oil or electricity to produce the heat; however, the economic difference is that the broody hen was expected to hatch and rear about fifteen poults each, whereas a modern brooder can cover from fifty to 250 poults.

In the early days of hand-rearing, the keeper required great skill to produce a correct diet for the young chicks. Protein was provided by rabbits, a young keeper on a large estate spending most of the rearing season catching, skinning and boiling them, and mixing them with hard-boiled eggs and barley meal to make a mash on which, it was hoped, the chicks would thrive.

These days, the millers produce a dry crumb which contains everything the chick requires. At four weeks, a pellet is introduced into the diet which contains less protein than hard corn but more of the important ingredients. At seven weeks, hard corn is mixed with the pellets and, over a two-week period, the poults are weaned onto a diet entirely of wheat. When the poults are seven weeks old, they are moved from their small brooder house and outside run into a release pen in the woods. The release pen has to be well sited so that the sunshine can dry the poults after wet nights. The size of the pen depends on the number of birds required in that area. One yard of perimeter wire for each poult is the recommended measure.

Where it all begins. A keeper checks his rearing field

To protect the poults from foxes and other predators, an electric wire is placed around the outside of the pen, about 18 inches from the perimeter wire and about 10 inches from the ground. After about three weeks in the pen, the poults will fly in and out at their leisure and the keeper will gradually draw them with food to the woods and the ride which will remain their home until shooting time.

A pheasant poult takes at least twenty weeks to mature and become sufficiently strong on the wing. When the pheasant season was introduced, 1 October was considered to be sufficiently early as this enabled the farmer with a few acres of root crops to harvest some birds before they wandered back to the large woods on the nearby estates. In these days of hand-rearing, 1 October is considered too early to start shooting as hand-reared poults take longer to mature than wild-hatched birds. On most shoots, the last week in October sees the first shoot day, when the boundaries and the outside coverts are usually driven in. This is often done by a few Guns walking the hedgerows back towards the middle of the shoot, taking the odd birds that are likely to travel over the boundary. When there are a few partridges, mallard, hares, rabbits and pigeon, in addition to the pheasants, these outside days can produce a lot of fun. On big shoots, a few beaters are usually employed and many more drives take place on these days than on the big covert days in mid-November. It is not until the middle of November when the leaves have fallen and the undergrowth has died away that the main covert shoots begin.

THE FIRST COVERT SHOOT

By this time, all the birds are fully mature, and the keeper has been feeding them into the places where they will produce the best sport. The beaters arrive early and, under the instruction of the keeper or keepers, drive the birds from the open fields, hedges and ditches into the wood. Then the Guns arrive. In this country it is customary for the shoots to begin between 9.30 and 10 a.m. whereas on the Continent they start at 8.30 a.m. There are normally four drives before lunch and two or three after lunch. In the shorter days of winter, a sitdown meal is taken at the end of the day and only a snack and a drink is taken at midday.

THE SHOOT MANAGER OR OWNER

The owner and the keeper have thoroughly prepared the order in which the various woods are to be shot. They have walked the ground days before and they both know exactly the plan of campaign. The shoot manager and the keeper usually place the numbered pegs or shooting stands at about 40 yards apart for the various drives.

When the Guns arrive on the appointed day, they are briefed by the owner on where they will be shooting and what they are allowed to shoot. Great emphasis is placed on safety and they are requested only to shoot 'when they can see sky'. They are also told where they may pick up with their own dogs, where the official pickers-up will be, and asked to move from stand to stand quickly and quietly (nothing disturbs game more than the human voice).

The Gun stands are normally numbered from right to left, with No. 1 on the right. After each drive, the Guns move up two places, i.e. No. 1 to No. 3 and, if there are eight Guns shooting, No. 8 to No. 2. It is customary for the Guns to draw for numbers before the first drive. The manager or owner instructs the Guns to observe the whistle which the keeper blows at the beginning and end of a drive. Nobody should fire a shot after the whistle is blown at the end of the drive, and guns should be unloaded and placed in their covers.

No dog is allowed to pick up during the drive; pickers-up with their dogs should be placed far enough away so as not to interfere with the shooting and to gather the birds which have fallen out of sight of the Guns.

THE SHOOTING DAY

After all the hard work of the summer and autumn, the day has arrived when the pheasants are ready to be harvested. After the briefing, the Guns are often transported by a four-wheel-drive vehicle or, in many cases, by tractor and trailer with bales placed around the outside of the trailer for everyone to sit on, to the first line of pegs. Having been allocated their number, they move off to take up their positions.

The first drive may be a long narrow wood and No. 8 Gun has to walk along the outside, level with or behind the beaters. At last the keeper's whistle blows, and the fifteen beaters move quietly, tapping their sticks against the bushes. The spaniels are in and out of the thick briars and the first cock pheasant rises and curls back over the walking Gun. There are two barrels and the bird flies on. The beaters move on quietly and thirty or forty birds are running along the top of the wood. The keeper is worried that George, who has been the regular stop at the end of this wood for twenty years, has not seen these birds and they have run along the hedgerow at the end

of the wood. However, there is a gentle tapping at the end of the wood and the keeper realizes that his faithful stop is in position. The beaters are now within 100 yards of the end of the wood. Two or three birds rise together and there is a flurry of shots. The keeper instructs the beaters 'take your time'. They all stop and he and the under-keeper move forward and rattle the laurel bushes. There is a flurry of wings and about twenty birds explode into the air together. Three curl back very high over the walking Gun, and he successfully pulls down a right and left.

The beaters progress another 30 yards and the keeper realizes that there is still a large number of birds in front of them. He does not want the syndicate members to shoot too many on the first day, so he allows thirty or forty birds to run back through the beaters. Gradually the remaining birds are worked into a flushing area. This time

A Gun waits as the line of beaters advances

Rising pheasant swinging through the branches

the keeper stops the beaters and moves ahead, gradually flushing two or three birds at a time. After several minutes of continuous shooting, there is silence, and eventually the keeper blows his whistle to end the drive.

There is great excitement amongst the Guns; the shoot owner or manager walks up to the keeper and congratulates him on a great show of birds. Most of the birds have fallen onto old pasture land and are swiftly collected, but two or three have run into an old lane where a lady with four labradors has been stationed to collect the runners and any birds that have fallen a long way out. Eventually she arrives with six birds and all eight Guns claim them. At last Reg, with the Subaru pick-up which is used as the game cart, arrives and he meticulously sorts the hens from the cocks and any damaged birds and ties them neatly in braces.

The second drive is from a field of roots on the home farm. A tractor and trailer have taken the beaters and keepers to the far end of the field, whilst the Guns walk the 200 yards to the first peg. They are lined out and within three minutes the keeper blows his whistle and the beaters zigzag through the roots. Nothing happens for 300 yards. Suddenly there is a flurry of wings and a covey of partridge rise in front of the end beater. As they fly forward, the Guns at the right-hand end of the line are taken by surprise. There are three shots but nothing falls. Suddenly, the keeper's old dog runs forward, eight pheasants rise, fly forward and sit on their tails as they see the Guns. Two or three of them break left and the colonel at the end of the line fires two shots and shouts to his neighbour, 'I think they're out of range.' At the end of the field several very young pheasants run onto the field in front of the Guns and the keeper blows his whistle.

Everybody is very excited because they have never seen roots on this field before. They wander back to the tractor and trailer and discuss how marvellous it would be if pheasants of the quality that came from the root field could be produced more often.

The last drive of the morning is the three-acre wood which never produces many birds. Nobody quite understands why because it is situated in

the sun and there is good holding covert. The beaters are lined out and have reached the final few yards before anything is seen. Two old cocks creep out, head high, but are not shot at. There is a shout from the owner: 'Those beggars have done that before!'

A cock pheasant retrieved. Gundogs play a vital role in a day's shooting

The whole party travels back to the keeper's house where his wife has produced her usual steak-and-kidney pie. The keeper and the beaters retire to the old stable and eat their sandwiches and drink their cans of beer in ten minutes; they have to wait another threequarters of an hour for the guns to reappear. Eventually they arrive and the tractor and trailer carries the whole party to the far end of the estate. There is very little here because the keeper refuses to feed his hand-reared birds into the small coverts as over the boundary is an unfriendly neighbour who has a very attractive field of kale. At lunchtime the bag was eighty pheasants and two

The drive is over and the birds must now be collected

rabbits. The shoot owner and the keeper have decided to shoot this less productive area because they have had such a good morning.

The first drive after lunch is a triangular wood known as Cuckoo's Acre. It is a mass of old elderberry and rosebay willow herb. The keeper luckily has two very brave spaniels and with their help eight pheasants are driven forward and three are shot. There are two more drives in the afternoon which produce another dozen birds and, at ten minutes to four, the keeper's whistle is heard and that is the end of the last drive.

The Guns, who have not seen each other since the previous January, have thoroughly enjoyed themselves and are looking forward to a very successful and enjoyable season. They agree amongst themselves that for a day of just over 100 pheasants, they should each give the keeper £7 as a tip.

HOW TO FIND PHEASANT SHOOTING

Most country boys who are interested in shooting are encouraged to go beating on their local estates. They get to know the keeper from an early age and volunteer to help with the rearing and other little jobs. They beat every shooting day and at the end of the season, when the owner or manager decides that his syndicate or guests have had sufficient shooting, the keeper is given a day for his helpers. There are often up to twelve Guns and they take it in turns to drive and to stand. For those in the country this is the first chance they have to shoot pheasants.

If you have a suitable dog and are keen to give it practical experience, go and see the keeper or owner in the summer and ask if you may come along on shooting days and pick up. You will meet people who might invite you to come and have a rough day.

There is far more opportunity these days to find shooting. There are many small syndicates who are looking for the odd Gun who has cash to contribute, whilst sporting magazines such as *Shooting Times* advertise shooting of all types to suit your pocket. There are also hotels which offer cheap out-of-season accommodation and have shooting rights.

COSTS OF SHOOTING

There are three main cost headings:

1. *Rent*. This varies over the country – in the southeast and near cities, the rent for shooting is very much higher than in the provinces. For a mixed woodland–arable estate within 40 miles of London, the rent can be as high as £2 an acre. In the remoter parts of Wales and Scotland, the rent might be only a few pence per acre.

2. *Keeper's wages*. These, as we all know, rise annually.

3. *Feed*. With the ever-increasing price of imported proteins which are needed for the laying hens, chicks and poults up to ten weeks old, the cost of feed has risen steeply in the last five years, as have wheat prices. In 1967 wheat was approximately £35 per tonne and in 1983 it was £125 per tonne. The cost of electricity, gas, keeper's vehicle, insurance has also risen.

On a well-run syndicate shoot, the cost of birds reared to birds shot is between £11 and £14 per bird. On the big commercial shoots where large numbers are reared, the cost is slightly lower and is approximately £11 a bird. Therefore a young man wishing to join a shooting party with an expected bag of approximately 100 pheasants can expect to pay from £130 to £150 per day, depending upon whether value-added tax is applicable.

In spite of these rising costs, the demand for pheasant shooting is increasing. Many syndicated shoots are letting one or two days a season to outside parties, often from overseas. It is very important that we, as owners or managers of some of the most beautiful countryside in the world, should continue to respect our privileges. Only such places as Hungary and Czechoslovakia can offer pheasant shooting to compare with that available in this country.

There is no more wonderful a sight than a winter's day with hard frost, weak sun and pheasants being driven across a very deep valley, the birds twisting and turning, the Guns pitting all their skills against the finest game bird. I hope that you, one day, will be able to enjoy such sport.

Rough shooter's delight – a cock pheasant collapses to the shot

ROUGH SHOOTING

Tony Jackson

Rough? Well, of course, it's not rough at all. Some of the finest sport to be found in this country – by hedgerows, in spinneys and copses, marshes and meadows, high ground and low – will keep one man and his dog fully exercised throughout the season. To hunt a cunning old cock pheasant, to walk up partridges on the stubble, to ambush pigeon flighting in to roost on a cold February evening or to tackle teal ripping through the dusk sky is to know the thrills and pleasures of genuine hunting. If, at the end of the day, tired beyond words, you have a pheasant or two in the bag and perhaps a handful of pigeon, you will experience the joy that comes from real achievement. You will have worked hard for every shot, there will have been successes and failures and occasionally the excitement of a bonus – perhaps an unexpected goose or a woodcock or golden plover. Best of all, you will have been working with an unquestioning companion – a gundog; perhaps only a rough shooter can establish the intangible rapport that can exist between man and dog, that fragile cord linking man and animal.

It is an individual sport. No talk of high-powered syndicates here, of formal driven days, of beaters and keepers and port-winey lunches; the bag will be modest but the sport and the sense of achievement will more than compensate. One man with up to three companions can, I fancy, be a rough shoot; more than this and you have a syndicate, with ambitious talk of release pens, reared birds and driven days. Certainly the rough shooter may improvise the occasional drive, perhaps to push a handful of pheasants over one or two Guns, but this is not what rough shooting is really about.

It is, of course, hunting in its truest sense. The bag has to be earned by hard work, skill and a gradually acquired knowledge of the countryside and its ways. Best of all, you will find yourself, often with only your dog, in the heart of the real country.

Your dog is your lifeline. Without a gundog you might just as well stay at home; your potential bag will be reduced by at least two thirds and, worst of all, you will not be able to deal with wounded quarry. Today, fortunately, nearly all shooting men and women recognize the vital role played by gundogs in field sports.

SOMEWHERE TO SHOOT

This is, sadly, the major obstacle facing the beginner and, regrettably, it is all too often considered as an afterthought. Inspired by the prospect of live shooting, our novice dashes out to the nearest gunmaker to expend a modest fortune on gun, clothing, boots, etc., and then, wonderfully equipped, dawns the horrid realization that farmers are simply not falling over themselves to provide him with a happy hunting ground. Rough shooting of any quality is desperately hard to find, though 'rubbish' shoots are fairly regularly advertised in the sporting press. 'Rubbish', because they will usually consist of a small acreage of impoverished land with about as much game-holding potential as the Arctic wastes. Such patches are often to be discovered close to large areas of conurbation and the fortunate owners are only too pleased to accept an extortionate fee in return for offering the privilege of a shot or two at the odd bunny or passing pigeon. Avoid such traps like the plague.

Of course, if you are lucky enough already to live in the depths of the country the problem may well be simplified for you, though a great deal depends on your personal approach and ability to make and use contacts. Even in the heart of the great game-shooting counties – most of East Anglia, Hampshire, Wiltshire and Dorset – patches of rough shooting do not come easily, but persistence always pays off.

Let's assume you have little connection with the countryside and that your purse has a limit. Somehow, if you are to gain access to some sport, however modest, you will have to make contacts and convince the locals that you are acceptable. Some astute groundwork is required. Nothing is for nothing in this world. Your rough shooting is almost certainly going to cost you these days. Before the war you might have obtained the right to shoot over 1000 acres for a couple of bottles of whisky at Christmas. Now, it may cost you anything from £300 to £1000. Certainly excellent rough shooting can still be found in far-flung parts of Wales and Scotland or even the West Country at a reasonable price, but most farmers and landowners are well aware that in or near more populated areas the demand for sport is high and the asking price corresponds.

Nevertheless, it is still possible to obtain rabbit, pigeon and vermin shooting at virtually no cost, provided the right approach is made. It is a complete waste of time to drive from farm to farm, the car laden with decoys, nets, guns and dogs, and expect a farmer to give you permission to range his fields. You may point out that pigeons are knocking hell out of his barley or rape and rabbits devouring his livelihood, but no farmer in his right mind is going to allow an armed stranger on his land without knowing a great deal about his background and credentials. You know that you would never leave gates open, let stock out or leave your empty cartridge cases littering the fields, while as for taking the odd pot at a pheasant – perish the thought! But does the farmer know? Besides, he is unlikely to be in a position to give permission. If, as is most likely, the sporting rights have already been let, he can only give certain members of his staff and family permission to shoot the ground game. In most cases the pigeon and rabbit shooting may have already been acquired by a local gun club on whose services the farmer knows he can rely.

But if you take the trouble to do some homework you may then be in a position to approach a farmer knowing something of his background, work problems and the names of a few local contacts who might vouch for you. Make use of that citizens' advice bureau of the sporting world, the village inn. Try to meet the local keepers and sportsmen. Use your ears and eyes and if you are offered the opportunity to go beating during the shooting season, don't turn it down. From such small beginnings you may find yourself master of several hundred acres or at least invited to join two or three other Guns on a modest subscription basis.

There is far more to shooting than firing a gun. Set aside a year in which to gain a real insight into how the countryside works and how its sports have evolved. As a rough shooter you will have a considerable advantage over the syndicate man who, once he has paid his subscription, may only see his shoot a dozen times in the year. You, however, will be deeply involved in gradually getting to know the countryside and its inhabitants. You will become knowledgeable in bird identification, in rearing and releasing game, albeit on a modest scale, and if you are fortunate enough to have water on your shoot you will also come to know and love the ways of wildfowl.

Clay pigeon shooting may seem an odd entrance to live rough shooting but I recommend you consider joining your nearest clay club. Not only will you learn to shoot safely and with skill, but you will almost certainly discover like-

Spaniels eager and questing.
Who knows what they may turn out?

minded sportsmen. Contacts will be made and invitations are sure to follow. The more rural and less high-powered the club, the greater are your chances of success.

There are also a number of wildfowling and rough shooting clubs scattered throughout the countryside. So popular is the sport that many, sadly, are forced to maintain waiting lists. How-ever, you can obtain full details from the British Association for Shooting and Conservation (BASC) at Marford Mill, Rossett, Denbigh-shire, the governing body for sport shooting. I need hardly add that, as a shooting man, it is essential you support BASC. Without their expertise and strength, shooting might have long since collapsed.

GUN AND CARTRIDGES

The rough shooter can be more catholic in his choice of armoury than, say, the driven game man or wildfowler. If his budget is limited, a sturdy single-barrel 12-bore – the Greener is an excellent choice – costing in the region of £100 will cope adequately with his basic requirements.

The obvious disadvantage of a single-barrel is its reduced firepower and, with most models, due to the rifle-like structure there can be a tendency to 'poke' instead of swinging freely when shooting. For pottering round the hedgerows after the odd rabbit or pigeon the single is a useful gun but you'll soon regret the single-barrel when you have a good day's pigeon

A goose may occasionally feature in the rough shooter's bag

decoying or a brace of pheasants clatter up in front of you.

Now I must admit to a prejudice, but one firmly based on years of experience. I dislike manually operated repeaters such as the slide-action or pump gun and the recoil and gas-operated automatics. Admittedly, the repeaters are usually rugged and hard-wearing, providing years of service, but they are basically ugly, ill-balanced guns, totally devoid of the simple advantages of a conventional side-by-side shotgun. In my view the latter, with its ease of loading, balance and pleasing lines, wins hands down. The English game gun is recognized world-wide as the peak of gunmaking; it provides the pattern for the finest gunsmiths of Spain, Austria and Italy. In its ultimate form, namely the 'Best' London sidelock ejector, it has scarcely been altered, or needed alteration, in a hundred years.

Side-by-side or over-and-under? The latter is now almost exclusively the choice of the clay pigeon world, but I do not think it has any advantage over the side-by-side; its very construction, with the barrels superimposed one on the other, demands a depth in the action which can create problems when loading, whilst trouble with ejectors is not unknown. Neither do I like the single-sighting plane. However, having made clear my preference, it is entirely up to the individual. I merely point out that the over-and-under is an unnecessary complication of an already tried and proven system. As far as clay shooting is concerned, one of the world's greatest exponents, Percy Stanbury, used exclusively a Webley & Scott side-by-side, fully choked in both barrels.

Boxlock or sidelock? The boxlock is the more common type of action. It fits into a solid action body, the springs running underneath the action. With a sidelock the lockwork is mounted on removable oval plates set into the sides of the action. A boxlock lacks these plates and tends to have a rather more bulky, less pleasing outline; it is, however, a simpler system. I would choose a cheap boxlock rather than a cheap sidelock.

You will hear a great deal of discussion about choke – either it is the ideal combination for a variety of circumstances or it is completely unnecessary. But what is choke? Quite simply, a constriction in the end of the barrel abruptly squeezes the charge of shot which is being impelled down the tube by burning gases from the cartridge. The effect is similar to squeezing the end of a hosepipe: from a gush of water one suddenly obtains a narrow jet.

Unfortunately, whilst increasing degrees of choke tighten the shot pattern and slightly increase the killing range at long distance, i.e. about 40–45 metres, at closer range a greater degree of accuracy is demanded from the shooter; game hit at moderate distances, though it will be dead, is also likely to be smashed and rendered uneatable. Choke is a dangerous animal, a snare and delusion for beginners, who imagine that maximum – full – choke increases their ability to kill at absurd distances.

Choke comes in varying degrees, ranging from true cylinder, which means no constriction, through improved cylinder, quarter, half, three-quarter and full choke. For game and rough shooting the best combination is improved cylinder and half choke. In a side-by-side the right barrel, normally the one fired first, will have the least degree of choke.

My ideal gun for the rough shooter is a side-by-side boxlock ejector, weighing about 6½ lb, with straight hand stock and slim fore-end, choked improved cylinder and half. Avoid pistol grips and beavertail fore-ends. They are out of place and unnecessary in a game gun.

When choosing a gun, balance it in both hands, slip it up to your shoulder and try to sense whether it is 'alive'. Handle a variety of guns to gauge the differing weights, balance and 'feel'. If possible handle one or two top-quality game guns. A Purdey or a Holland will feel alive in your hands and almost come to the shoulder by itself. An ill-made, cheap gun will feel dead.

Whatever your choice, don't put your signature to a cheque until you've taken expert advice. Never, under any circumstances, purchase a gun second hand until you have had it approved by a gunmaker. Remember that all guns, new or second hand, must have passed proof in Birmingham or London, and that, when sold, they must still be in proof. A gun which is out of proof used with a normal load, or, worse still, a load which is excessive may burst, causing grave injury or even death.

Fortunately, there are today fewer guns on the private market and one seldom comes across the real horror – out of proof, rusty, off the face and cracked stock – the sort of gun which can be tarted up by the unscrupulous dealer to catch the innocent.

As for cartridges and loads, moderation in all things is the keyword. Most beginners fall into the big load trap. The heavier the load, the more shot they can cram into the cartridge, the better they like it. A 1-oz or 1$\frac{1}{16}$-oz load is perfectly adequate for virtually all contingencies in this country, and if you stick to No. 6 or No. 7 shot you will not go far wrong. Heavy magnum loads are the province of the foreshore shooter dealing with long-range duck and geese and have no place in the rough shooter's battery.

The only exception to the above remarks is when shooting hares. I dislike shooting hares but that is a personal phobia. If you know that hares are likely to figure in the bag, arm yourself with No. 4 shot. A wounded hare is a pitiful sight; never take long shots at hares. They can absorb a surprising amount of shot and are quite capable of escaping with a broken limb.

SAFETY FIRST AND FOREMOST

As a rough shooter you will constantly be encountering situations which demand particular attention to safety. Gates must be climbed, ditches crossed, wire negotiated; companions and dogs will frequently be out of sight and their exact positions not known. You have a loaded, lethal gun in your hands, an instrument which, at close range, can inflict the most devastating damage on soft tissue and which, even at 200 metres plus, is capable of putting out an eye. To give yourself some idea of the destructive nature of a shotgun, fire a game load, an ounce of No. 6, at a tin can 10 metres away, then imagine the same effect on a human body.

Safety rules are simple and rely entirely on common sense. Only a gun which is pointed at a person is capable of killing or wounding. Never, under any circumstances, point a closed gun at anyone. You may know it is empty; the potential victim does not and one day you will make a mistake – the gun will be loaded. Always break the gun and remove the cartridges when crossing an obstacle, when not shooting or expecting a shot, or when on or in a vehicle. The old school of game shooters maintain that a shotgun should be carried closed between drives – an open gun might strain the action or allow moisture into the lockwork – and that one should rely implicitly on the good sense of one's companions. It was, and is, an unacceptable and potentially dangerous act.

There are two correct methods of carrying your gun, alone or with companions. Either over the crook of your arm or on your shoulder, trigger guard uppermost. Do not carry it at the trail, on your shoulder with the trigger downwards or, worst of all, across your body. Don't hesitate to point out his faults to anyone you see engaging in these potentially dangerous acts.

EQUIPMENT

Even for the rough shooter lacking the formal demands of the driven game man or specialist requirements of the pigeon shooter or wildfowler, there are still basic items of equipment which will be required. Of course you can wander round in jeans, wellingtons and a tweed jacket, but you will make life much easier for yourself with clothing made for the job. My own choice for winter shooting is a pair of loden breeches, lightweight green boots, a thorn and waterproof jacket and a soft hat or cap. I also carry a sidebag for game and a cartridge belt. Loden breeches are extremely durable, soft, warm and almost waterproof. Slightly more expensive than cord or tweed breeches, the extra cost is well worthwhile. Breeches with a pair of stout, thick socks are much to be preferred to trousers which, if they become wet, cling to the legs. In dry weather a good pair of leather boots will offer more comfort than rubber boots. You should also buy a pair of waterproof overtrousers, an absolute boon in thick cover.

A woodcock is always a notable feature of the bag

Most important of all is a comfortable waterproof, thornproof jacket. There is an extensive range of these on the market, most of which are variations on a theme. The more you are prepared to pay, the better the lining, the waterproofing, the fastenings and closures. It is a good plan to acquire an absorbent choker made of towelling. On a rainy day this will prevent water trickling down your neck.

As far as headgear is concerned, avoid the Sherlock Holmes type deerstalker; you will be far better off with a soft brown trilby or tweed cap.

You will need a strong sidebag to carry the game. The traditional gamebag has a netting container on the outside. Avoid this at all costs. Game crammed into netting is quickly crumpled and ruined. I much prefer a simple canvas bag with a broad leather strap. An ex-postman's bag is ideal.

MAN'S BEST FRIEND

Shooting on your own without a dog is like eating eggs without salt. In order to put game in the bag, you *must* have a reasonably proficient gundog, an animal which will both find the game for you, retrieve it when shot and pick up any wounded birds which might otherwise have been lost. You're not looking for a field trial winner; it does not have to put on a polished performance – dropping to shot, retrieving perfectly to hand – but it must *not* run in to shot or chase flushed or bolted game; it should be capable of basic handling, it must retrieve without mangling or eating the game, and should walk to heel and sit when told. These are the basic requirements and from them will stem the refinements which add so much to the pleasure of working with an intelligent, enthusiastic companion.

The choice of a gundog – what breed, whether dog or bitch – is a personal matter, but there are some guidelines to be followed. As a rough shooter, you will demand an animal capable of both hunting and retrieving your quarry; versatility is the name of the game. Labradors and golden retrievers are both superb dogs within the compass of their intended activities but you cannot really expect either to hunt a thick hedge or patch of brambles with the enthusiasm and energy of an English springer or a cocker spaniel.

A good spaniel, on the other hand, will demand additional qualities from its handler. It is full of fizzing energy and frequently headstrong; you can seldom let the dog get on with the job without a degree of supervision. You really have to keep on top of a springer spaniel otherwise you will swiftly discover that the dog has taken charge of the situation. The great joy of a quality springer is its enthusiasm and total commitment to the task facing it. Always with a spaniel there is hope. The most apparently blank piece of cover may still, it seems to say, hold a cock pheasant or rabbit. Optimism is the spaniel's great forte.

On the other hand, for combining the qualities of hunting, pointing the game, flushing and retrieving it when shot, one of the increasingly popular breeds of pointer–retrievers, the German short-haired pointer, is, in my view, the ideal rough shooter's dog. I have owned labradors and spaniels but for four years have worked a GSP, and a more intelligent, sensitive and delightful working dog I have yet to encounter.

The pointer–retriever breeds (which include Vizslas, Weimaraners and Münsterlanders) all stem from the Continent and have largely become popular with sportsmen and women in this country since the last war. Apart from their versatility in the field, they have the advantage of being free from the inherent diseases which are now plaguing labradors in particular.

They do, however, have a reputation for hardmouth. This, in fact, is a gross slander and any tendency towards rat-trap jaws can usually be avoided by making sure that the young dog is not permitted to retrieve wounded game in its first working season.

Whatever your choice of gundog, do not, I plead, buy the first puppy that is offered. Take some time to examine the market and avoid the locally bred, backyard litter. They may look charming and cuddly but, equally, their background may be deplorable. Nonworking show parents are fatal. I cannot emphasize too strongly the need to avoid any taint of show blood in the pedigree. Far better to approach an established working kennel and, if possible, take along someone who has a broad knowledge of working pedigrees. Ask to see one or, if available, both parents demonstrated and then pick the pup you like the look of. At ten weeks it is almost impossible to choose a puppy which will combine all the virtues. However, if it is bred right from disease-free stock – and make sure you ask to see a certificate guaranteeing both parents free of hip-dysplasia and retinal atrophy – and it is trained with commonsense, you should have an invaluable working companion for eight to ten years.

If you are going to train the dog yourself, buy a practical book on gundog training and follow its instructions implicitly. The golden rule is to hasten slowly. Take each stage of training at a modest pace and make sure that the dog fully grasps what it is being taught before advancing to the next stage. Most novice trainers tend to rush basic training to get on to the more exciting business of hurling dummies and firing shots. That is fatal.

Trainers who tell you their young dog of six or eight months can do everything including play the piano are only fools to themselves. A dog bought as a puppy in the spring of the year should not be entered to live shooting until it is some fifteen months old. Rush the real thing and you may ruin months of work.

Nothing is more infuriating than an ill-behaved dog in the shooting field. Sport will be ruined and tempers rapidly frayed as it charges about, oblivious to whistle and voice. It is not the dog's fault but that of the owner who has proved incapable of training it to a minimum acceptable standard. And what is that standard?

The dog should walk to heel when told; it should stop on the whistle and be capable of

Man and dog working in harmony

A mixed bag – mallard, pheasant and woodcock

being handled at a distance; it must not, under any circumstances, run in to shot and it must retrieve cleanly. If it is capable of performing these functions without drama and fuss, you will have a dependable working companion, the envy of your friends.

PUBLIC RELATIONS

Always remember that whenever carrying a gun you are in a position of trust. Misinformed or uninformed members of the public may take exception to your activities. If you are verbally attacked you must be armed with facts; as a sportsman, participating in an age-old and legitimate sport, you have a sound case. You are a guardian of the countryside and will undoubtedly have a greater stake in furthering the interests of its wildlife, albeit for your own ends, than the casual rambler who simply fails to understand how the countryside works.

At the same time, make sure that your behaviour is invariably impeccable. Don't go outside the law, however tempted you may be on occasions. It may appear innocuous enough to shoot a marauding sparrowhawk taking pheasant chicks, but you may be seen and, for a short-term benefit, you will have done neither yourself nor the sport any good.

The rough shooter has, I believe, the best of shooting worlds. The sport he enjoys is worked for and created by himself. He is in constant touch with the countryside and will come to know and understand its moods and whims. He is to be envied.

Red deer stags offer a unique sport in the Scottish Highlands

DEERSTALKING IN THE HIGHLANDS

Lea MacNally

In Britain the term deerstalking refers almost certainly to the pursuit, with the rifle, of red deer in the Scottish Highlands, a sport unique in the fact that the red deer live on the bare rocky heathery hills, devoid of tree cover. This lack of cover makes Highland red deer fascinating animals to pursue. Using optical aids such as a stalking telescope or powerful binoculars, you can, with due care, especially when the rut is under way in October, spend an enormously interesting day, without firing a shot, simply watching deer activity – and this amid magnificent mountains which can rival scenery anywhere in the world.

There are also glimpses of interesting wildlife to be had – fox, wildcat, otter, mountain hare, golden eagle, peregrine falcon, grouse and ptarmigan. Combine this with the glow of achievement in successfully getting up to a keen-sensed wild animal, far more at home in the mountainous terrain than you are; the sheer physical effort involved, the miles of wild country walked over, and you begin to understand the aura of content which surrounds a stalking party returning from the hill with a stag on the pony.

In front, wending its way down the glen, the ghillie-led pony, the stag, finely balanced, swaying atop the deer saddle in time to the pony's gait over the uneven ground; behind, the tired but supremely contented stalkers. Therein lies the varied and lasting charm of deerstalking in the Highlands. In this small and overcrowded island of ours, in which we have long ago disrupted the balance of nature, there are areas of wildlife remaining which, in order to conserve, we must also control. Conserving a species implies conserving its habitat. Where an excessive number of grazing animals is permitted to occur, serious damage to their habitat inevitably ensues, and this in turn leads to a decline in the animals' living standards. Since in Britain today we have no significant natural predators such as the wolf to limit the number of our adult red deer, their control falls to man. Deerstalking, while a fascinating sport, is also a management tool necessary to control the annual increase in the herds and to ensure their wellbeing.

I believe the emphasis in stalking red deer should be on culling the inferior animals of both sexes and ageing deer. Where there are enough good heads in the stags to justify this, some trophy heads may be tried for annually. Similarly in the hind-stalking season a limited number of good-quality beasts may be taken for specific reasons. In the long term the wellbeing of the herd will repay this kind of policy.

EQUIPMENT

Despite the wide range of synthetic-fibred clothing available nowadays, the traditional suit of tweed is hard to beat for deerstalking. Tweeds were, after all, designed for use in stalking on the hill and long usage has proved their worth. My preference is for the shorter plus-four type, or indeed knee-fastening breeches. Since hill walking is now a widespread pastime, many shops keep a good stock of ready-made knee-length tweed breeches, so there is no need to have an expensive tweed suit made. A camouflage jacket completes my outer garments, together with woollen stockings. Make sure that your jacket is not of a fabric that rustles noisily when you are in the last crawling or wriggling stages of a stalk. Deer have extremely good ears. The virtue of tweed clothing is that it is virtually noiseless as you snake, belly to the ground, among heather and rocks. Moreover, even when wet, tweed retains some warmth and is comfortable.

Whatever outer garments you choose, avoid very dark or very light colours. Loden cloth, a favourite with stalkers on the Continent, while ideal for stalking in the shade of coniferous woodland, is unsuitable, because of its dark green colour, for most northwest or central Highland deer forests where the overall background colouring in autumn is a warm orange-tawny hue because of the predominance of fading autumn grasses. You may get away with darker clothing in the northeast Highlands where the hills are predominantly heather-clad; remember, however, that dark clothing becomes even darker when rain-soaked and can appear black. Black stands out on the hill. Consider the range at which one can see a stag which has just blackened his coat by wallowing; he is much more obvious than a red-coated beast. The remedy is in your own hands; choose a drab shade of russet brown, fawn, grey or a lighter green, or, better still, a mixture of these colours. Take a tip from the deer; their coats blend well with their surroundings.

Some kind of headgear is essential; the pink-white disc of the human face is very apparent amid heather and rock as it rises to peer at deer, and a cap or deerstalker with a peak helps shade this. A cap will also serve to subdue unruly hair which may attract attention as you worm in over the last bit of your stalk. Nothing is calculated to attract the attention of red deer eyes more than movement where all should be still, and hair blowing about on an uncapped head may mean

the difference between success and failure. Equally a cap will subdue the highlights of the bald head of the more mature stalker.

Footwear is supremely important. Miles of rough and varied terrain varying from the soft and boggy, through leg-entangling, strong, rank heather or ankle-testing, tussocky, tough grasses, to rock-ribbed ridges, can be very hard on footwear. Burns and rivers have to be forded. Above all, do not choose a stalking day to try a new pair of shoes or boots. I remember stalking many years ago, with a man who, in the course of a long day, suffered such a crop of blisters that he actually stopped and padded each boot with wool from the highly pungent carcase of a dead sheep. Don't risk such a drastic remedy. Try to combine lightness with comfort – whether boots or shoes. I always advise rubber soles of Vibram or commando-type. The alien clink of metal carries far on the hill and the ears of the deer are quick to detect its warning. On a very wet hill, and this is common in the west Highlands, I favour a pair of green-coloured, flexible, light hunter wellingtons. Wear a larger size than normal and make up the fit either with an extra pair of woollen socks or Bama sockets.

Carry one or two extra hankies or, better, a supply of soft paper tissues in a plastic bag. These ensure that you can dry off your telescope, binoculars and telescopic sight. Remember wet weather is the rule rather than the exception on the autumn hills.

No matter how hardy you believe you are, carry a pair of gloves. Warm fingers are much more sensitive to trigger feel at the vital moment than fingers numbed with cold. I do not like carrying a bag on the hill, my preference is for roomy pockets in which to put my lunch, etc., but, if you must, choose a small haversack rather than a rucksack. The human figure is bulky enough when trying to emulate the worm, without carrying an extra hump on its back.

For the Highlands, the traditional stalking telescope is still the best when deerstalking; × 20 magnification means that you can select or reject the quarry at a much longer and therefore safer range than when using binoculars. Many people who already have binoculars may not wish to acquire a stalking glass, but do remember that without one you will have to do more walking to examine each group of deer, and this will entail greater risks both in having to make a close approach and when withdrawing if there is no suitable beast in the group. If binoculars are the choice, leave the case behind and carry them under your buttoned or zipped-up jacket. Use lens caps (if you have not already lost these!) as protection against rain and snow.

Your knife can be of the pocket or sheath variety. Always choose one that is strong but not too bulky or weighty, and in the case of a folding pocket knife ensure that it has a locking device when open so that it does not unexpectedly fold shut on your fingers. Should your choice be a sheath knife (as mine is) make sure that it fits tightly in its sheath; you will be crawling, slithering sideways, wriggling, sliding on your back, over all types of rugged terrain during a stalk. The loss of a prized knife is bad enough, the discovery that you have a deer to gralloch and no knife to accomplish this with is even worse. In many years of stalking this has happened to me

on several memorable occasions. I have had to make do with a sharp-edged flake of rock, the metal tang of my belt and a pair of nail scissors found fortuitously in a pocket. I have known of an empty cartridge case being used, its brass beaten flat between two rocks. Believe me, it is much easier with a knife! As a last word on this, do not make your choice on appearance, or on the apparently lethal quality of a knife; rather, make sure that it is comfortable in the hand when in use and not too heavy.

Carry a length of thin strong rope, but avoid nylon. Nylon rope is exceedingly strong, but it is very hard on the hands on a protracted drag. You can, of course, drag a dead deer by its antlers, or by its legs, and on very steep ground this may well be adequate. Over long flats, however, a length of rope is essential for dragging your deer to pony or vehicle.

Your most important piece of equipment in deerstalking is, needless to say, your rifle. Calibre is largely a matter of preference, but .240 is the minimum which should be considered for use on red deer. Over the years I have tried

Glassing the hill. In deep snow, a stick is an aid in using the glass

Climax of the stalk – a steady aim and a careful shot

calibres of .240, .243, .244, .256, .270, .275, .303 and .300 and I have found all of these adequate. Having settled on .243 as my preferred calibre, I do not intend to change from this now. There is choice enough nowadays for every taste. If you feel that .243 is inadequate for a stalking rifle, then choose .275 or .270. Having settled on one particular combination of rifle and bullet weight (mine is .243 and 100-gramme bullet), stick to this, become accustomed to it, know its capabilities, and do not chop and change unnecessarily. As with so many tools, it is the man behind the rifle that dictates its best use, within obvious limits. Remember also that if you change your bullet weight it is wise to check your telescopic sight *before* using it on a live target.

Your choice of sight is, again within limits, a personal matter. Telescopic sights are the rule now, and as the purpose of any rifle sight is to ensure accuracy in achieving a clean kill, they have the advantage. My choice in the wide range of telescopic sights now available, at a wide variety of prices, is one of ×4 magnification with a fine cross-hair reticule. An improvement on this type available now is one in which thick cross-hairs lead to a central fine cross in the centre. There are many experienced stalkers, however, whose preference is for the post-type reticule, finding that it is easier to see in poor light. Variable-power (up to ×10) telescopic sights are also readily available at a price. These seem particularly popular with stalkers on the Continent. This type of scope sight is, I feel, quite unnecessary; ×4 is adequate and needs no adjustment. Have your scope sight mounted as low to your rifle barrel as possible and remember that this mounting is every bit as important as your scope. A mount which periodically, and usually haphazardly, goes off zero is liable to let you down when you need it most and is not to be used on a living target.

Scope sights are delicate, precision instruments and as such *must* be treated with care. Try to avoid bumps, knocks or falls. If you slip while on the hill, try to cushion your rifle in preference to yourself – unless you are teetering on the edge of a precipice, of course! Check its accuracy at the beginning of each season and if you do sustain a fall, or accidently knock your rifle and scope, check its accuracy at once. Wounding an animal and then having to follow it up with the inaccurate rifle can be a harrowing experience. Many modern rifles do not have open sights, so that one is entirely dependent on the accuracy of the scope sight.

A word on open sights. My preference is for the peep, or aperture, sight. Of the V-type sights, the wide, shallow V or U is best. Sight your rifle in at a range of 150 yards; with modern flat trajectory rifles, this ensures accuracy at the desirable stalking ranges, which may vary from 80 to 150 yards, with, occasionally, a slightly longer shot. Don't be tempted into very long shots; the skill in deer stalking is in the approach work, *not* in long-range Bisley-type target shooting. Always bear in mind that deer are as capable of feeling pain as you are, if more uncomplainingly.

Use a flexible cover when carrying your rifle to the hill and for most of the stalk; this will serve to protect it from knocks and grazes on harsh rocks. It will also be extremely valuable on a sunny day in preventing the metallic parts heliographing your approach to the deer. A pair of end caps for your scope sight is a great asset, nay an essential on a wet day, for that crucial last few minutes when your rifle is out of its cover. The panic-stricken hanky or paper-tissue-fluttering attempts to dry off a scope sight which is opaque with moisture, while under the mildly inquiring gaze of a stag, is neither conducive to your calmness nor to the success of your stalk.

A final word on your rifle. Become absolutely familiar with this until it becomes an extension of yourself. The climax of a long, skilful, exciting day's stalking can be brought to nought by unfamiliarity with your rifle. Fumbling at the last moment may cause a panicky, overhasty shot, resulting in a miss or, worse, a wounded beast. Your stalk has taken time, skill and effort; do not nullify all this at the last moment. Take time and studied care over your shot and learn to reload as a reflex action in case a second shot is needed. The best of marksmen cannot shoot effectively with an empty chamber.

THE STALK

Equipment sorted out, now to the stalk. To enjoy stalking under Highland conditions, you must be fit enough to withstand strenuous walking over rugged mountainous terrain in all kinds of weather conditions. Even to get to where you may reasonably expect to see deer you may have to walk a mile or two. Having arrived at your red deer ground, the first essential is to choose a commanding viewpoint and, without risk, especially of exposure on a skyline, sit down and spy the ground in view, paying most attention to wind-sheltered corners where deer may be lying inconspicuously, chewing the cud. This cautious spying *has* to be repeated whenever fresh ground comes into view; you are looking for deer, deer may well be looking at you. It only needs one carelessly alarmed deer to clear miles of hill, deer after deer picking up the alarm telegraphed by a single animal until the entire area is on the boil.

Having found a suitable quarry unalarmed, the stalk must be painstakingly planned and here an all-important factor is the wind. You may deceive the eyes and the ears of deer but never their noses. The gentlest zephyr of wind, barely ruffling your neck hairs, blowing from you in the direction of those infallible noses, and you are lost. Deer disturbed by the unmistakable scent of man will also go farther than if only alarmed, yet not entirely convinced, by the sighting or hearing of 'something' suspicious.

Having made sure of the general direction of the wind (an upward glance at the carry of the clouds is valuable in this), the rest is basically commonsense. Choose a line of approach which will take you, unseen and unheard, as near to your quarry as necessary for the shot.

The best way to approach deer, if wind and terrain allow, is to come in from above, even if this means a lengthy detour and a steep climb. Deer lying or grazing on steep ground seldom face directly uphill and their view in this direction is restricted. The stalker has the added advantage of a better view from above and usually a better firing point. Never forget that your approach must be planned to avoid disturbing intervening deer and/or sheep.

In some deer forests prevailing winds may dictate an approach from below. In these cases there is usually more crawling work, and belly-to-earth wriggling, to add to your enjoyment and suspense. At other times you may be able to 'slice' the wind, i.e. essay an approach from one side of the wind, exercising fine judgement in edging in without the wind betraying you, keeping it on your flank rather than heading directly into it.

The last stages of any stalk are always critical; overeagerness and very natural impetuosity must be guarded against. Deer are most easily approached when grazing, most difficult when lying, resting, chewing the cud. Should any one of a group suddenly cease this rhythmic chewing and, pricking its ears, gaze intently your way, this means suspicions aroused. Do not confirm these suspicions by immediately jerking back into better cover. Instead, freeze absolutely, no matter how awkward your posture or how agonizingly protracted the period. Chewing resumed means suspicions allayed, and this is your cue for shrinking, ever so slowly, back into cover.

A common weakness to guard against is that of concentrating all your attention on your selected quarry, particularly in the last vital few yards. You may miss the sudden fixed stare which indicates undue interest on the part of another in the group until it is too late. *All* deer are watchful, not just the one you want to bag. Watch them all and in those last few yards be extra cautious.

When crawling, avoid elevating your rump while conscientiously scraping the heather with your nose. The sight of the human rear, disem-bodied as it may appear, progressing like a camel's hump above the line of a sheltering peat hag will send deer away. Similarly, when wriggling flat to the heather, draw your entire body flat behind you; don't propel yourself by digging your knees in and consequently telegraphing your approach by a pair of lower legs flailing in the air. When unavoidably exposed to the gaze of deer, move infinitely slowly; this type of movement can deceive the eyes of deer whereas quick, jerky ones draw their gaze. Leave your wristwatch at home or have it in a pocket; its flashy exposure as your jacket sleeves ride up in crawling may relay warning of your proximity.

Be very slow and careful in sliding your rifle into position for the shot and in exposing your cap-shaded head. If there is a convenient hummock, slide your way into position beside it rather than suddenly breaking the skyline on top of it, tempting as it may be as a rifle rest.

When using a scope sight do make sure that your rifle muzzle is clear of rock or ground ahead. You may have a clear picture through your scope but your muzzle is lower than this.

Point of aim on your deer is a matter of experience. A neck shot is very satisfying, lethal and quick, yet it is not a certain shot unless one is close enough (say 80 yards) and skilful enough to be able to break the neck. A stag's hairy-maned neck looks a big target but most of this is non-vital. You may miss through the mane or, worse, you may put a nice clean but non-vital perforation through the windpipe. My preference is for the lung shot, which is lethal and speedy. Point of aim for this is just behind the foreleg and midway up the body. For the heart shot, again aim behind the foreleg but only a third or so up the chest as the deer stands broadside.

Never attempt a head shot in profile; this presents a large area of non-vital head, the lethal area, the brain, being barely the size of an orange. A hit in the lower jaw or nose means an excruciatingly painful wound and the shot deer will run at once, to die maybe days later; the risk is not one to be accepted lightly by any stalker worthy of the name.

When a deer is lying down it is better to wait until it rises, unless you are near enough to try

Stags in winter when subsistence is at its hardest

for a neck shot. A recumbent beast may be 'persuaded' to rise to its feet, *if all else fails*, by a grunt, a whistle or a simulated roar at rutting time, but this can be risky if overdone, resulting in the precipitate departure, usually rump on, of your quarry.

After your shot, reload instantly *and be still*, watching your deer. Correctly shot through the lung, it will flinch perceptibly, perhaps walk a few steps, begin to sway, fall and die. It may even run a few yards before beginning to sway, but it will not dash forward galvanically as deer shot through the heart may do. Only when your beast is down and unstirring for several minutes should you slightly relax your readiness to take a second – *coup de grâce* – shot. If, at the shot, your deer drops like a stone, be extra vigilant – this *may* only be a spinal crease or graze (and this applies to neck shots), the deer being momentarily stunned. The sight of a 'dead' deer up and

running after you have congratulated yourself and have stuffed the rifle back into its cover is indescribably mortifying. If you have shot too high and broken the back of your quarry, the deer will struggle desperately but unavailingly to rise, and a speedy second shot is called for.

A shot too far back in the body is often signalled by a loud smack or thump as the bullet hits the large fodder-filled stomach. In this case the beast will usually exhibit a hunched-up, dejected posture and after a moment or so walk slowly off. A quick *coup de grâce* is again called for, but above all *do not* let a beast so wounded get a glimpse of you when trying for the second shot. A deer apparently near to death can summon amazing reserves of strength to evade you if it sees you.

Should you wound a deer, remember it is incumbent on you to follow it up until you get it, or until you are satisfied it has only a superficial

81

Dragging a beast off the hill

Loading a stag on to the deer pony

graze from which it will recover. It is better for your peace of mind, however, to do everything that is humanly possible to make sure that your shot *is* lethal.

All having gone as it should do and having watched your prone deer until you are sure it is dead, and until its companions have gone, you now have to clean it out and to get it back to the larder. For the required gralloching, i.e. the removal of stomach and intestines, roll the dead deer over onto its back. Stand astraddle the chest, facing the tail, and with the edge of your knife make a small preliminary incision just below the end of the breastbone, taking care not to go too deep and so puncture the stomach bag. Insert two fingers and raise the skin clear of the underlying stomach bag, re-insert the blade of the knife and, guided by the two fingers, slide this down to the pelvic area. Roll the deer onto its right side. You will find that the insides will partially roll out of their own accord through the incision. Push both hands in above the spleen, which is attached to the large stomach bag, and you will readily remove stomach and intestines. It is not necessary to bleed a dead deer in the traditional manner; instead, open the skirting skin dividing chest from abdominal cavity, and drain out all the blood. Heart, lungs and liver are left inside for removal at the deer larder later.

Your gralloched beast must then be dragged to where it can be loaded onto the deer saddle of a pony or into a vehicle of sorts. Over short distances, deer can be dragged by antlers or legs; for longer distances the length of rope should be used attached to the head. My own system is to slit the space between the strong V-angle of the lower jaw with my knife, insert the rope and make it fast.

Should you be using a pony to get your stag back, you will also most probably have the assistance of an experienced ghillie who will know how to load the stag. The pony will carry one stag or two hinds. When loading a stag, it simplifies matters if it can be laid on a suitable bank or large rock. The pony is then brought up so that the deer saddle is nearly on the same level. The stag can then be part-lifted, part-slid onto the saddle, haunch first.

The antlered head is secured first, being bent hard back to lie along the upper part of the dead stag's chest and tightly bound by a strap. A single strap at each end balances the carcase for what may well be a long journey home. Properly balanced, the saddled stag *should* look as if the haunches are hanging too far down on their side of the saddle. An adjustment or two to girths or straps may be necessary before you reach the larder. If the pony is of the fidgety type, a jacket over its head while loading can be an advantage. Hinds, being lighter and without antlers, are simpler to load, two to a saddle, using one strap at chest and one between haunches for each hind.

Finally, when deerstalking, always remember that your rifle *is* a potentially lethal weapon. Only load it on the hill with the prospect of a shot imminent. Unload it when the day's stalking is over. Count each round as you unload and, as a final safety measure, poke your little finger into the chamber of your empty rifle. 'Empty' rifles have gone off before now, creating due consternation and utterly spoiling an otherwise enjoyable day. Deerstalking the Highland way has, however, an extremely good record for accidental shootings. Keep it this way.

Always remember your duty to the deer you are stalking; your object is a clean kill and no suffering. Achieve this and you will sleep better at night after a day's stalking.

Stalking is *not* an inexpensive sport. You can expect to pay something in the region of £150 per day to stalk a stag, exclusive of accommodation, and it is usual to express your appreciation to stalker and ghillie in the form of a tip at the day's end. Overtime rates are not paid to stalkers or ghillies and I have known a party as late as midnight back at the larder, though this is exceptional. For hind stalking the daily fee in 1983 was £40–£50, again exclusive of accommodation. There are many well-established sporting agencies which offer deerstalking facilities, some through the medium of *Shooting Times and Country Magazine*.

It remains only to wish you good stalking. I am confident that it will be memorable.

Beagles and beaglers – the Holme Valley move to a fresh draw

BEAGLING

Rex Hudson

'Going hunting' – those two evocative words mean widely different things to different people. For those of us who live in towns and cities it often conjures up a Christmas-card-like image of men in red coats on horseback with hounds outside a traditional country pub, a motif often vying in popularity with the stagecoach or ubiquitous robin. For a great many people who live and work in the country, however, hunting has been both a sport and a recreation for centuries, as well as an opportunity to meet friends and neighbours. Above all, hunting is a way of maintaining a healthy, ecologically balanced population of wild creatures. This latter point is often ignored by the opponents of hunting, who lose sight of the fact that all wild creatures – mammals, birds and fish – are not a constant, fixed population.

'Conservation' is a very popular word these days, and is applied to wildlife, old buildings, whatever, but conservation is not static in its effects. The conservation of wildlife in all its interdependent forms means the sensible husbandry of all species within a harmonized environment wherein they breed and have their being.

Any collection of wildlife species is constantly changing – old animals past their prime are replaced by young, fitter ones – and hunting plays an important part in the sensible control of wildlife resources. Young, fit hares are easily able to evade hounds, whereas old, diseased ones are caught and quickly dispatched. There are no geriatric homes for old hares and the alternatives to hunting – snaring, trapping, poisoning, etc. – are unacceptable to most right-thinking people.

Why is control necessary? It has been estimated that ten hares eat as much in the way of field crops as a single sheep; and the damage done to forestry plantations can be considerable.

It is against this background, therefore, that we consider the question of beagling which, along with angling, has become increasingly popular throughout the British Isles in recent years. Why this has come about is not difficult to understand. Like angling, it takes a person with a natural interest in the subject out of his or her home or work environment, requires only a minimum of 'formal' training, and provides an absorbing, fulfilling and healthy exercise. Beagling does not demand good horsemanship or a large bank account. It embraces people from all walks of life, all ages and from widely contrasting backgrounds. They come together, bound by a love of sport and an interest in wildlife and the countryside.

In its basic form beagling consists of three elements: the hare, the hounds and the spectators, usually known as the field. It is to be found over widely differing areas of country, of which the British Isles has such variety. There are packs of beagles hunting in marshlands, on uplands, mountains, moorlands and even in woodlands, and the sport is conducted according to strictly enforced rules of good sportsmanship and behaviour.

To many, the hare, beloved of nursery-book illustrators, seems to be a timid, indeed timorous, creature, and hunting her* with hounds is thought of as despicable; the fox, on the other hand, is perceived as a cunning creature, largely due to his undoubted ability to obtain his living at the expense of the hen yard. In fact, both species are very resourceful and soon acquire a knowledge of the area in which they live which is quite exceptional. The hare especially combines a courage and a pugnacity that can astonish the casual spectator.

It is for these qualities that, from pre-Roman times, the hare was considered the premier beast of venery, possessed of great speed, cunning, agility and subtlety. She is admirably fitted for the life she leads and, whether in agricultural regions with arable crops or on plough or grassland countries, adapts well to her environment. The same qualities also make her a worthy sporting adversary, especially when pitted against a pack of small hounds inferior to her in speed, knowledge of the country and a host of other factors.

The hare is a born survivor. She has to be. From birth she spends her life above ground. Born fully furred and with open eyes, the leveret lies concealed in her form in a secluded spot selected by the mother, with her few brothers and sisters similarly concealed within close reach. Many of these leverets provide an easy meal for any predator that comes upon them, so the survivors reach adulthood with an inbuilt sense of self-preservation accorded to few other animals. Superbly camouflaged, the hare nevertheless has an attractive scent which puts her life constantly at risk, quite apart from making her eminently huntable. However, nature provides that when she is immature, heavy with young or suckling, her scent is virtually nonexistent. (In any case, hares are not hunted during breeding time.)

* For some reason hares are invariably referred to as 'she', irrespective of sex, in much the same way as foxes are always called 'he'.

Young hares are at first suckled by their mother, visiting each in turn. As soon as they are weaned, they rapidly become self-reliant and quickly acquire a knowledge of the surrounding countryside. As she develops, each hare extends her territory, so that by the time she is adult she is probably familiar with many hundreds, perhaps thousands, of acres. This knowledge will probably stand her in good stead one day.

Her degree of mental and physical fitness and her sense of survival combine to give the hare the important place she has had in the world of hunting for nearly 2500 years. Indeed, although when hunting is mentioned, most people new to field sports perhaps think first and foremost of foxhunting, despite the British love of horses and the thrill of riding, often at high speed over difficult country, foxhunting as a popular sport is relatively young, being about only two or three hundred years old.

In all forms of hunting, the newcomer often becomes confused about the various types of hound and their relative sizes. The height of the hound is usually determined by the size and speed of the quarry. Foxhounds, which stand 24–25 inches at the shoulder, are perhaps the best known. Then there are staghounds (27–28 inches) and harriers (19–21 inches); coming right down the scale, beagles and basset hounds vary from about 13 to 16 inches at the shoulder. The type of country hunted by the pack also has a bearing on the size and height of the hounds, a fast grassland country being hunted by lighter and smaller hounds than those used over heavy plough or steep hills, which make great physical demands on hardworking hounds.

Both beagles and bassets – which are used for hare hunting – have become very popular in recent years as household pets and as show dogs. The working beagle generally resembles its urban brother, although the standards of the show bench differ in some respects from those required in the working hound. The show hound, to which most pets are related, is invariably selected on one criterion: its conformation, assessed according to the standard laid down by the society fostering the breed and recognized by the Kennel Club. The working hound, on the

Basset hounds – low on leg but high on perseverance

other hand, is a complex mix of *performance* qualities: drive, determination, a generous nature, stamina and good old-fashioned guts. It must keep its head down and hunt the line on a wet, cold, blustery November day; it must have a soft, receptive nose – scenting ability is what hunting is all about – and a good voice to tell the world, particularly its pack mates, what fun this hunting business is. Above all, it must be able to hunt as part of a team on two or three days a week during the season, perhaps covering between 20 and 30 miles a day over varied country. All these and other attributes are welded together in a conformation which enables each hound to fulfil its role in the hunting field with the minimum of strain.

The working basset comes in two forms: the pure-bred, rendered popular by its appearance in a well-known footwear advertisement, and the so-called English type, which is closer to the beagle in height although somewhat heavier in general conformation. The latter carries a proportion of harrier or similar blood in its make-up. The qualities sought in the basset are the same as those required in beagles, and both types of hound acquit themselves equally well in the hunting field.

The hunting season officially begins in early November but, in arable areas, early morning hunting, when the young hounds begin to learn their part in the sport, starts as soon as the corn is cut. The pack – which usually consists of ten to sixteen couples* – is hunted on foot by a huntsman with perhaps two or three assistants or whippers-in.

*The hounds are grouped in couples for easy counting when they check or are being collected.

Beaglers must take the country as it comes

Blowing for hounds

The huntsman's job is to 'draw' likely areas where a hare has been seen or is believed to lie. He encourages the hounds with his voice and his horn (although the latter is used more to inform the field of his actions when out of sight) to seek diligently for the scent. When hounds approach an area where a hare is sitting, she invariably tries to slip away. Occasionally the hounds will see her, but ideally they should keep their heads down until they come upon her scent and, with a wonderful burst of music, as the cry of the hounds is called, proclaim their find.

At this point the first part of the huntsman's job is largely completed. He now has to make the best speed he can to catch up with the hounds, which, in the initial stages of the hunt, have probably outdistanced the huntsman, the whippers-in and the field. Sooner or later, however, the hounds check, and it is at this point that the hunt staff should be in touch with them. It is important that the hounds are reliable and do not go after livestock on those occasions when they are out of touch with their huntsman or his whippers-in.

The whippers-in keep an eye out for any hound that might become a straggler or detached from the main body of the pack. They must also watch out for railway lines and busy roads where there is risk of injury to the hounds. One of the fleeter-footed whips may try to get ahead to see which way the hare has run, but by and large the matter of the pursuit lies between the hare and hounds. In many cases the best efforts of the huntsman and the whippers-in are a neutral force, or even a negative one. Indeed, a cynic once said that beagles tend to hunt in spite of

89

their huntsman rather than because of him, although few huntsmen would agree with this.

Sooner or later a check occurs, and then the hare frequently displays her proverbial cunning. To elude the hounds she will sometimes make a prodigious leap through a hedge or run along the top of a wall to throw the hounds off her scent. The hounds then either cast themselves or if the huntsman is with them, he will cast them himself. This means that the pack swings in a circle around the spot where the scent was lost in the hope that they will hit off the line and start to hunt as a body once more.

There may be anything from four to twenty or more checks in the average hunt, depending on the scenting conditions, which in turn are controlled by temperature and humidity.

The culmination of the hunt has two forms: either the hare is killed or she escapes altogether. If she is eventually overtaken, the leading hound will dispatch her, much in the way a terrier does a rat, by a clean snap at the nape of the neck. In the majority of cases, however, the hare escapes and returns to her home area. It is estimated that only one out of every four hares hunted is killed.

So far as the field is concerned, the spectators can take as much or as little exercise as they think fit. In the early part of the season, the hare tends to run in a very large circle. This means that the younger or more active members of the field can run behind (never in front of) the huntsman and his staff, while the older or less active can take themselves to the nearest high ground from where, with field glasses, they can watch the hunt taking place below them. Because of the hare's propensity to seek out rising ground where her superior speed and long hind legs make it easier for her to outdistance her pursuers, the watchers on the hill may well get a sight of hare and hounds at close quarters.

Whether the field member is active or inactive, the rules are the same: the hare must always be given every possible chance of escape; she must never be flustered or interfered with in any way. If a member of the field sees a hare running towards him, he should throw himself flat on the ground and remain immobile if possible, or freeze so as not to distract her.

As one gains experience in beagling, the question so often asked by the novice as to how the huntsman knows one hound from another is answered. Each hound, apart from its appearance, has characteristics and behaviour patterns that distinguish it from its pack mates. One will excel at hunting the line of a hare over a road (a very valuable characteristic, this), another will hunt through kale, for example, in a way that can be recognized by the huntsman who may only be able to see the extreme tip of its tail ('stern'). The individual abilities of each hound must be known by the huntsman. Like humans, hounds differ from each other – some are truthful, some tell lies; some work hard, others shirk. It is important, for example, that a working hound can be relied on when it opens on the line.

One of the greatest joys of beagling is to know each hound individually by name. Keep a notebook and write down the characteristics of two or three hounds each hunting day. In this way, all members of the pack will in time become familiar. With this knowledge, if a hound 'goes missing', as sometimes happens, a member of the field may be able to help the Master or whippers-in to find it.

In addition to the pack in the field, there is a number of hounds back at the kennels which will perhaps hunt on other days. Each pack hunts on average two days each week during the winter months. The hounds have to be looked after, exercised and so on for the remainder of the year; an important time is the breeding of young hounds in the spring. The majority of puppies from working hounds are retained in the pack or drafted to other packs to replace older hounds that have passed their prime. As soon as they are weaned, the pups are 'walked' by farmers or members of the field, who look after them for about a year. By the time they start hunting they are about eighteen months old and fully mature. Whilst at walk they will have learned their names and, with luck, not to chase cats or chickens. By the time they return to their home kennels, they should be ready to settle down as working members of the pack.

Visitors are invariably welcome at the kennels by appointment, and experienced field members

A member of the field views a hare away

Hounds in full cry

The puppy show, climax of the year for puppy walkers

are sometimes allowed to help exercise the hounds or carry out other chores. The majority of packs hold a puppy show each year where the young hounds that have returned from their walkers are shown and prizes awarded. This is usually an occasion for a social gathering such as a teaparty where friendships made in the hunting field can be renewed.

The hunting of the hare in the field is conducted in accordance with the rules laid down by the Masters' Associations. Any breach is severely dealt with, a Master risking expulsion for a proved infringement. Few parts of Britain have not been registered by one pack or another, and a Masters' map is maintained, which shows the boundaries of all hunt countries. Any new pack wishing to hunt in unregistered country must first obtain the consent of the Master of Foxhounds in the area, and then the agreement of the Masters of foot hounds with adjacent boundaries. At present there are some eighty-seven packs of beagles and eleven packs of basset hounds hunting in the British Isles, which means that there should be a meet within easy reach of anyone with access to a car, bus or bicycle. Meets are advertised each week in *Horse and Hound* and *Shooting Times*. Anyone wishing to locate their nearest pack should either make inquiries in their district or contact the relevant Masters' Association which will put them in touch with the Master of their local pack.

As to costs, members of the field are expected to pay a cap for a day's meet, usually anything from £1 upwards. If you wish to hunt regularly, you will be expected to pay a subscription; these vary from pack to pack. The cost, however, is probably less than the membership fee for any other type of club.

Clothing does not need to be elaborate or expensive. Anything that is warm, waterproof and permits freedom of movement is suitable. Stout jeans, thick socks and training shoes seem to be favoured by the younger generation. If you have a car, a change of clothes and a towel in the boot is a good idea, as you will be going out in the winter and will probably get wet and cold on many occasions.

There is a wealth of good beagling literature. Most libraries have up-to-date books on the subject. Specialist booksellers will also have from time to time second-hand copies of older works, many of which are still eminently readable and relevant. Here again is the charm of beagling, based on a love of natural history, of the countryside, and of the traditions of our sport.

Beagling has remained virtually unchanged for 2500 years. Certainly there are modern hazards – motorways, traffic fumes, railways, artificial fertilizers – but these tip the balance in favour of the hare, rather than the hounds. Those of us lucky enough to be a member of a beagling field are watching a chapter of history – our history – of a sport which will never die so long as there are hares to enrich our countryside and gallant little hounds to delight us with their voices, their companionship and their gameness.

USEFUL PUBLICATIONS AND ADDRESSES

Weekly magazines

Horse and Hound
Shooting Times and Country Magazine
The Field

Hunting associations

The Association of Masters of Harriers and Beagles
Hon. Sec. J.J. Kirkpatrick
Fritham Lodge, Lyndhurst, Hants

Masters of Basset Hounds Association
Hon. Sec. Rex Hudson
Yew Tree Cottage, Haselton,
Cheltenham, Glos

Booksellers specializing in beagling and hunting

R.E. Wey
Brettons, Burrough Green,
Newmarket, Suffolk

J.A. Allen & Co.
Lower Grosvenor Place,
Buckingham Palace Road,
London SW1

Loneliness of the empty shore

WILDFOWLING

Arthur Cadman

What is wildfowling? In its purest form it is the pursuit of wildfowl on the foreshore between high tide and low tide. This includes some of the wildest and loneliest places in Britain, and wildfowl – wild geese and duck – are amongst the wariest of the quarry species. Success is infrequent and bags are usually small or, much more often, nothing at all.

So why go wildfowling? The magnet which draws a fowler into the teeth of a winter's gale, to leave a warm bed long before daylight and trudge through mud and water in the dark to reach the place of his choice before dawn, is very similar to the force which compels the mountaineer to attempt the most difficult climbs, often enduring terrible weather, to gain the summit of a mountain, which may, sometimes, be reached by an alternative easy path or even a mountain railway! It is a challenge, and in modern life there are too few real challenges to take you to the wilderness areas.

To those who live in cities the foreshore means a crowded beach, warm weather, white gulls wheeling against a blue sky, and waves lapping the feet of children. Why should anyone wish to shoot a poor defenceless bird under such idyllic, peaceful conditions? Every wildfowler would agree with this sentiment, for the summer scene and butterfly weather coincide with the time when his guns, well oiled and spotless, are stored away in his gun cabinet.

Come with me to some of the real wildfowling areas, the vast saltmarshes of the East Coast or the great expanses of the Solway, where a wildfowler, if he were a flea on a snooker table on a similar scale, would not have time to reach the mid-point of the table before the next tide sent him scurrying back! Let us in our mind's eye see the great Kent flats, or the bare mud of the Humber estuary, and scores of marshes around the shores of Britain. No paddling children, paunchy old men in deck chairs or even topless beauties here!

So, let's look out over one of the great East Coast saltings on a sunny evening in July, six weeks before the duck-shooting season starts. We stand on the seawall (only the inexperienced do that during the open shooting season!) and at once a redshank rises screaming abuse. Near the seawall the sea lavender shows mauve, and indeed the saltmarsh flora is of great interest to the naturalist.

A muddy creek wanders through the green marsh, and a lone curlew, bubbling its lovely liquid call, flies down the creek to settle a quarter of a mile away, disappearing from sight. (That same creek can become a hazard during a winter's flight with a racing spring tide!) Three-quarters of a mile from us the saltings tail away, changing to mud. Here, at this time of year, grows the green samphire, a cellular plant delicious to eat.

Far out on the mudflats there are shelducks, two old birds with nineteen young, the offspring from several broods. A big bunch of mallard stand, heads under wings, on a sandbank beyond. That is where the pinkfeet, the real wild geese, will roost come October. Soon those mallard will flight inland to feed on the ripening wheat inside the seawall. Farther out is the white line of the tide spilling over the flats, with vast clouds of waders wheeling and flying to and fro,

Arthur Cadman

glinting silver in the sun. If the tide was not on the make we would see mud for as far as the eye can scan – thousands of acres of mudflats and sands, which, like most of the saltings, are covered twice in every twenty-four hours by the sea.

Massive changes take place. Sandbanks disappear overnight and, of course, different levels of the saltings are covered by seawater for different lengths of time, according to whether the tides are making towards the height of the spring tide or falling towards the much lower neap tides. Spring tides coincide with the times of the new and full moon, and the neaps with the intermediate periods. They also vary with the strength and direction of the wind.

So conditions are rarely constant for long. They change with the state of the tide, and the state of the tide changes each day, and this is also affected by the degree and direction of the wind. All these things affect the behaviour of wildfowl. Apart from that, the time of year, which influences the different feeding areas and the effects of migration, which in turn may control the number of wildfowl in the area, also affects the local fowling conditions.

As a general rule, duck and geese flight at dawn and dusk; but duck feed by night and rest by day, whereas geese do the opposite. So, at dawn, duck will be returning to the shore, where they may spend the day, whilst geese leave the shore and flight inland to their feeding grounds. Some species of duck and geese will flight under the moon and a moonflight of pinkfeet, or of wigeon, is the cream of all wildfowling.

There are many complex considerations which the wildfowler must understand before he can be in the right place at the right time. 'Hope and expectation' provide the urge which spurs him on. Disappointment today will lead to extra hope tomorrow – for he will have observed where the wildfowl have flighted today. Tomorrow he will be there – but local conditions may have changed and he may be wrong again!

That is the mystique of fowling, the why and the wherefore, the application of personal knowledge based on observation, and above all the hope that tomorrow will be *the day*, and that, at last, one will be in the right place: it is all these things, plus the love of wild places, the sights and sounds of the wildlife which inhabit them that is the essence of wildfowling.

EARLY DAYS

The raw beginner, standing with his most useful piece of equipment – a pair of field glasses – beside the old weather-beaten local fowler, will wonder how he can set about shooting wildfowl in these great, wild spaces with all the complications I have mentioned. Let us assume that he is a member of the British Association for Shooting and Conservation (BASC), that fine organization which looks after the shooting man's interests (and the interests of the wildfowl which he hopes to shoot), and that he has joined a local wildfowl-

Setting out a raft of decoys

ing club, which allows him to shoot subject to the club's rules.

He has so much to learn and the best way is to go out with an experienced fowler as many times as possible in the close season, listening to what he says, observing the tide, watching all the birds, wildfowl and others, which inhabit the shore. He must learn to identify the quarry species and as many as possible of those which are protected – otherwise his sport will be greatly curtailed, for

the rule which he must observe at all times is: '*If in doubt – don't shoot.*'

He must have a set of tide-tables (only a fool goes fowling without knowing exactly what the tide is doing, otherwise, one dark winter's night, he may float in feet first – and that causes a lot of trouble for so many other people!) and he must learn the effect of different winds upon the tide and understand all about spring and neap tides. Then, when he has gleaned as much knowledge

Decoys can be very effective

as possible from the experienced fowler, he must set about getting to know every part of the marsh and shore. He must follow the creeks through the saltings and study very carefully which ones will cut him off from the seawall when the tide is on the make. He must note high banks where he may be able to hide at low tide (even a 2–foot bank provides good cover!)

If he is dismayed at the formidable task of learning the ground, the effects of the tide, the habits and movements and identification of the wildfowl, and much more, then he will never make a wildfowler. Let him give up and return to a cosy fire and the 'box'.

But if, when he reaches the seawall, his nostrils dilate with pleasure at the tang of the saltings, if the wild cry of a curlew and the chattering of redshank are music to his ears, if the distant sight of mallard dropping down to the mud thrills him, then he has caught the wildfowling bug and never will he be cured! Then he will be caught up in the mystery of migration, the mystique of bird movements, the wonder of all that he sees. 'Where have they come from and where are they going?' He will ask himself the eternal question a hundred times and mastering some of these things will give him the impetus to go out in the worst winter weather – just to see if he is right. And, if he is right, and if he holds his gun straight, and if he has a good dog, he may return with a couple of fat duck or – the height of achievement – a wild goose! That achievement may represent many, many hours spent waiting and watching with only the companionship of his dog (which, despite all its faults, will be the best dog in the world for him!)

So do not let the emotional 'poor defenceless bird' people think of wildfowling as the slaughter of the innocent! It is a great sport, a demanding sport, where the main attraction is to be 'out there' with a great deal of 'hope and expectation' and often very little else, except a bootful of mud and seawater.

Suppose, for one moment, that one day you open your back door and see a thousand sparrows. That would be quite a sight! But, in goose country it is nothing to see twice that number of geese. The sight of two or three thousand pinkfeet flighting inland off the estuary, lines and Vs of geese crossing the pink dawn, whilst the clamour of their wild music fills the ear with wonderment – that is one of nature's great spectacles! The wildfowler, perhaps a mere speck on the mud half a mile away, may be the only witness to this supreme sight. He will return all the better for having seen them – and eat a huge breakfast. One day he will be in the right place!

There are many considerations which people who are not naturalists do not understand. The number of any species depends upon many factors, but the prime one is their habitat. The habitat for a species will support only a certain number. After a successful breeding season there is a surplus of juveniles, some of which will replace winter deaths of adults. The remainder must either find a new habitat (in most cases it does not exist), or fail to breed, or perish. Many perish. (Of some species, e.g. grouse, nearly all the surplus dies of disease or starvation.)

The sportsman, whether wildfowler or inland shooter, takes a fair harvest from the surplus, and those that remain are all the healthier because they are able to feed better during the lean periods. Shooting and conservation go together, as the title of the BASC indicates. Were it not so, there would be very little left to shoot! But it is not as simple as that. Most shooting people are good countrymen and good countrymen understand much of the very complex pattern of nature and delight in encouraging and preserving rare species – not in order to shoot them if they become plentiful, but because the countryside would be worse off if they no longer existed.

All these things and, particularly, good sportsmanship must be learned by the novice. He must see that his sport does not interfere with others – whether wildfowlers, bird watchers or those whose livelihood depends upon the countryside. Above all he must learn to respect his quarry. Long chancy shots, however tempting, must not be taken. Very soon he will discover that just being out with gun and dog in the wild surroundings of the foreshore is what it is all about. What he sees with his field glasses will come to count as much as what he shoots.

EQUIPMENT

When a newcomer to the sport of wildfowling sets out to equip himself he will find it a great temptation to be overequipped. So what are the essentials?

First he must have a pair of field glasses. Without them his pleasure will be curtailed and his knowledge of wildfowling will be limited. 7×50 or 8×50 are the best, of robust construction.

He needs thigh waders. Often it is necessary to crouch down and waders keep the knees dry. They should be large enough to take an extra pair of thick stockings or Bama linings.

A waterproof jacket that comes *below* the top of his thigh boots is essential. There are many excellent thornproof coats on the market. A waterproof deerstalker hat, which shades the face from being seen, and prevents the neck from

acting as the top of a rain gauge, is best, unless one is shooting from a lying position, in which case the back rim gets in the way. Gloves with the right finger cut off are desirable.

A home-made canvas 'goose bag' is better than a smart game bag. It needs to be waterproof and capacious. Its main use will be to sit on! I have mentioned tide-tables – keep them clean, at home. A compass and a whistle are also essential.

CHOICE OF GUN

I have left the question of which gun to the last because, although it is of prime importance, it should only be chosen after a reasonable degree of knowledge about wildfowling has been obtained.

If you already own a game gun, then you can use it for fowling provided you take great care of

A fowler takes a gutter in his stride

it – every gun, even the cheapest, requires not only careful handling, but also looking after and cleaning with scrupulous attention to detail. The advantage of using your game gun is that you are already used to it and therefore will shoot better with it than with a gun that you only handle infrequently. But some shooting people can pick up any gun and shoot equally well with it. They are lucky!

There are many snares and false illusions in choosing wildfowling weapons. Nearly every beginner falls for the temptation to acquire a heavy magnum, fully choked and loaded with large shot. Like so many, I have gone through this stage. There was a time when I thought that nothing smaller than No. 4 shot, fired through a full-choke barrel, was 'right' for ducks. Long ago I had my guns, even my 3-inch magnum, bored out to improved cylinder and quarter choke.

The point you have to consider is that if you use full-choke guns only, you have to hold straight that little bit more accurately. Often you get only one or two chances at a flight – and it is easier to miss with a full-choke than with the wider pattern of a more openly bored gun. Then, once in a while, you are lucky enough to experience the flight of the season. There is a gale blowing, you are in the right place, and duck are coming low. A heavily choked gun is a great disadvantage then. All too often you return home with your tail between your legs, dismayed that you have missed so many, and horrified to find that some of those shot duck have been smashed. How much better, when that very rare flight comes, to shoot well, with your game gun loaded with No. 6 or No. 7, and to carry back completely undamaged duck in your bag!

So what do you choose? I recommend the purchase of the best-quality gun you can afford, with 2¾-inch chambers, and with neither barrel bored full choke. At fair range, 35 yards, you will kill all the duck you need with 2½-inch No. 7 shot. If there is a chance of geese, then use 2¾-inch cartridges. My personal choice is as follows:

For duck coming to a flight pond, or on a tight flight line in a gale: 2½-inch cartridges, No. 7 shot. For average wildfowling on the shore: 2½-inch, No. 7 in the right, 2¾-inch, No. 4 in the left. If the geese come, usually there is time to change the No. 7 for heavier shot. For geese only: either 2¾-inch No. 3 in the right and BB in left or, the same in a 3-inch magnum. (In theory BB gives too open a pattern. In practice I, and many friends, find that this size gives such a clout that it is most effective!)

INLAND FOWLING

So far only the shooting of wildfowl on the shore has been covered. But there is much wildfowling to be had on the great inland river systems, marshes, lakes and lochs, flood waters and even small pools. Some of the inland shooting, especially the shooting of hand-reared mallard, or duck coming to heavily fed flight ponds, is not really wildfowling. It may be called 'duck shooting'.

There is a case for rearing mallard, but the intention should be to put something back into the wild, to replace some of the wild stock of the area which will be shot during the course of the season. If hand-reared duck can be established so that they learn to flight like their wild cousins, then this is excellent, but it needs skill to release them so that this happens. All too frequently they become too tame. The sight of tame mallard being chivied about in order to make them fly over a team of (probably) equally overfed and lazy guns is one which every wildfowler deplores.

But shooting duck when they have learned to go wild on a large lake or local estuary is perfectly acceptable. There is the interest of looking for a ring or wingtag on every duck that is shot. Could that tall duck that flared up as your gun came up, and none the less fell dead, really be the one you reared, ringed and released 2 miles away?

On the opening day, last season, a keeper friend brought off a right and left at two mallard out of a small bunch that came over him on the edge of the shore. They both carried rings. To my surprise they were a duck and a drake, bearing consecutive ring numbers, which some years previously I had reared and released a considerable distance away!

Out of 100 mallard established safely on the shore in one year (except for two or so that were killed by predators), only seventeen were shot. But the number of mallard breeding the following spring in the general area was greatly in excess of normal. That is the result that the hand-rearing of duck should give.

Flighting duck inland can be most exciting. There is the same hope and expectation as the day slowly fades. But the background is different, and often more difficult than on the open shore, for duck are not easy to see against trees or distant hills. The sights and sounds of the countryside are different from those on the shore, but equally impressive to senses alert with anticipation. Partridge calling on the stubble that, not long ago, was a golden sheet of grain; pigeon cooing in the wood beyond the marsh; a cock pheasant 'cock upping' as he goes to roost; perhaps a flock of long-tailed tits or siskins working through the tops of the alders before the light fades and drives them to roost; the call of a moorhen or the thumping of a rabbit. These, and many other such country things, hold your attention, so that when the first bunch of teal suddenly drops in from nowhere you are caught unaware. All these are part of the inland duck-flighting scene.

Then there are the morning flights – the excitement of finding your way in the dark to the hide at the edge of a large lake and the sound of the wind in the reedbeds, the whicker of wings before it is light enough to see; perhaps most exciting of all, the quiet chuntering of geese out in the middle of the water. That makes the pulse quicken.

After the flight is over, if some fowl have come over your hide, and if the gun has been held straight, there is the happy accord with your dog as he searches for, winds and retrieves what you have shot. On the open shore a dog either has very easy retrieves of duck lying on the mud, or very difficult retrieves from water, or from a long way off, of the odd wounded goose or duck. Inland the dog may have to swim, but quite often his skill is needed to find fowl that are concealed in dense undergrowth or wide reedbeds.

The other exciting form of inland wildfowling is to shoot geese coming to the fields on which they have been feeding. That can be very

exhilarating. But sometimes, when decoys are used and conditions are right, it can be too easy. Under such circumstances every true sportsman will impose a limit – either a bag limit, or a time limit. After that, let him slip away quietly and leave the geese alone to return to feed in peace.

CONSERVATION

Wherever you shoot wildfowl, inland or on the shore, you will find a great spirit of friendship between like-minded sportsmen. Such friendships last a lifetime and the tales of success, or failure, will last long into a winter's night! One of the great needs of wildfowling today is to build up a spirit of friendship with those who do not shoot. It is important that they should understand more about wildfowling, just as wildfowlers need to understand their point of view. Only by such cooperation can the proper conservation of wildlife – which both desire – and the future of wildfowling survive the pressures of modern life. The natural balance between plant, insect, bird and beast, each in relation to its own habitat, is most complex. What the selfish shooting man must realize is that overexploitation can be harmful; what the non-shooting conservationist must appreciate is that proper harvesting of the surplus helps preserve the habitat from overexploitation by its own inhabitants. And the judicious control of predators – carrion crows, magpies, rats, mink and foxes – benefits many other species as well as those which in winter provide the quarry of sportsmen.

It is important that every shooting person should know the law that controls the open seasons and the species which may be shot. The shooting of game birds is controlled by the game laws. The shooting of wildfowl is controlled by the 1981 Wildlife and Countryside Act. Details of this are complex and it is recommended that a summary of the relevant parts is obtained from the BASC or from the RSPB.

Finally, what reading will help the novice (and the experienced) wildfowler most? There are many books on the subject, but the best one is: *The New Wildfowler in the 1970s* (Barrie & Jenkins, 1970). No other book covers the whole

Dawn and dusk are the wildfowler's hours

Geese – the fowler's chief quarry

subject so well, and in such excellent detail. It was one of the BASC's (then WAGBI) contributions to the European conservation year of 1970.*

In the foreword, His Royal Highness the Duke of Edinburgh, who describes the book as splendid, writes:

> The book is primarily about wildfowling but it is also about conservation and as such I hope it will be read by people who are interested in conservation but who are not necessarily wildfowlers.
>
> The pressure on all forms of wildlife is so intense that the only hope is for all groups interested in any aspect of the conservation of wildlife and wild places to act in concert.

No other words could have put this better. And in his preface, Sir Peter Scott describes vividly what wildfowling is about, and emphasizes 'that enjoyment in wildfowling bears no relation at all to the size of the bag'.

Let every newcomer to the great sport of wildfowling uphold and honour the traditions of unselfish, good sportsmanship, respect the quarry he seeks to outwit, and foster good relations with those who do not shoot, but who also love the wild places and the wildlife that inhabits them.

DON'TS

1. Don't forget to set your alarm.
2. Don't forget to refer to your tide-tables.
3. Don't leave your bed without knowing where you intend to go.
4. Don't park your car where it will interfere with farmwork, farm stock, farm machinery or other people.
5. Don't carry your gun between your car and the shore other than in a gunslip.
6. Don't come tearing out onto the shore after, or during, duck flighting time and disturb everyone and everything (in other words, get to your place in good time – or stay away).
7. Don't be selfish, greedy or inhumane.
8. Don't take up your position too near other fowlers or stand unconcealed where you will turn every goose from everyone.

*At the time of writing, this book is unfortunately out of print.

9. Don't forget to look through your barrels before loading and, when on mud or snow, at very frequent intervals. Burst barrels do not give very good patterns!

10. Don't ever forget to handle and use your gun 100 per cent safely, always, everywhere.

11. Don't fire your gun unless you know that the bird at which you aim is *not* protected, *not* out of season, *nor* out of range.

12. Don't shoot at any quarry beyond the capacity of your gun, your ammo, or your skill.

13. Don't shoot at any bird which will fall where neither you nor your dog can hope to retrieve it.

14. Don't let your dog run all over the shore, bark, fetch the only duck someone else has shot, pick a fight with another dog, or jump into someone else's car, whether covered in mud or not.

15. Don't leave any wounded bird unpicked until you are *sure* that further search is useless.

16. Don't leave what you have shot lying in a heap in your garage. Smooth the feathers and hang the bird in the game larder as soon as possible.

17. Don't forget to dry your dog and clean your gun before you see to your own comfort.

18. Don't forget to encourage the novice – but don't tell *everyone* exactly where you have had your best flight.

19. Don't hesitate to speak your mind to those whose behaviour brings the sport of wildfowling into disrepute.

20. Don't forget that every fowler has filled his boots, and when your turn comes, it is good for a laugh. (And if you lie on your back and raise your legs without turning down the tops, you'll get a lot wetter where it matters more!)

He who reaches his three-score years and ten and can say, perfectly honestly, that he has never once transgressed in any one of these points is a paragon who should be stuffed and put in a glass case. But that is no reason for not trying to comply on each and every outing.

Aerobatics by a high speed grouse

DRIVEN GROUSE

Tony Jackson

Lagopus scoticus, the red grouse, is the one game bird with which the non-sporting public can immediately identify. The Glorious Twelfth is the sole shooting date in the calendar known to the media and the public, and arouses, every year, a minor spate of uninformed comment and unintended humour. The images persist, the fusty ghosts will not be laid. Ask the man in the street to react to driven grouse and the moors, and he will instantly conjure up a small army of mottled colonels in voluminous hairy tweeds or bemonocled chinless wonders performing some esoteric rite amidst a blaze of royal purple heather.

There is, so we are told, no smoke without fire and, of course, the public mental picture is based on elements of truth, but it is now a far cry from reality. You are far more likely to find a posse of Americans, French or Germans manning the butts as the packs of grouse sweep across the moors. Today, grouse moors are big business and sporting foreigners readily recognize the unique atmosphere and the undeniable fact that driven grouse probably offer the most exciting and the finest sport in the world.

It is not a cheap sport – the best things in life seldom are – but if the opportunity ever arises, if you are invited to shoot, cancel all appointments, don't stop to think twice and head north. Of course, grouse shooting can be obtained at modest rates but it will usually be walked-up with dogs or, far more intriguing, over pointers and

setters. The shooting will not be difficult, the birds will offer relatively simple going-away shots, but to be in the presence of bird dogs which know and understand their business adds a new dimension to the sport. Given the choice, I almost prefer a day's dogging to driven shooting. The bag will be small, you will have walked a fair few miles but you will have been privileged to watch the aristocrats of the dog world working as they were intended to do. A red setter, gliding across the heather, working the ground and using the wind, finally locking on to point, is a truly magnificent sight. So too is an English pointer, every muscle carved and rigid as it catches a whiff of grouse scent. These are moments you will treasure when all the rest is long since forgotten.

There are four species of the grouse family in the British Isles – the ptarmigan, a hardy bird confined solely to Scotland and seldom found below 2000 feet; the blackgame, a handsome bird, the cock a glossy blue-black with a lyre-shaped tail, the hen a drab grey, also found south of the Border; the capercaillie, the largest grouse of all, the cock weighing up to 12 lb; and, of course, the red grouse.

It was once believed that the red grouse was unique to the British Isles, but it is now accepted that it is in fact related to the willow grouse of Scandinavia, but with the distinction of failing to adopt the latter's snowy plumage in the winter. There appear to be types of red grouse, for you will come across three distinct colour phases – rufous red, white-flecked and nearly black, with various colour combinations in between.

Grouse are found principally in Scotland with the main populations in the east and central Lowlands, in the north of England, and even as far south as Shropshire where there is a moor on the Longmynd south of Shrewsbury, in north Wales, whilst there is a tiny remnant population on Dartmoor and Exmoor. They are also to be found in Ireland, though here the bird is sadly in decline.

Like the ptarmigan, the red grouse is a tough, hardy bird which survives and thrives under conditions which would be a death warrant to many species. Its staple diet is the shoots and seedheads of ling heather, the bloom of bell heather, grass seeds, wild berries and corn; it also needs a supply of grit and water. Grouse will consume insects and, where heather is deficient, will make do with crowberry and rushes.

Unlike pheasants and partridges, grouse are totally wild and their population is not supplemented by reared birds. In order to thrive, however, they are dependent on rigorous moor management. The basis is correct and carefully applied burning of the moor on a rotational basis to stimulate young, nutritious growth. A moor which never sees a flame will be almost useless for a healthy population of grouse: the heather will be ancient, long-stemmed and lacking in food value; grouse chicks will become lost in the jungle of stems; and it may also harbour ticks.

The burning of a moor is not just a question of haphazardly setting fire to vast areas; strips of two to six acres will be fired and the burn carefully controlled. It sounds relatively easy but in practice the weather and the labour force available are the dominant factors. A well-managed burnt moor will appear from a distance as a series of rectangular patches of fresh growth.

Burning is only a part, though a major part, of the moor keeper's tasks. Access to the moor, the maintenance and construction where necessary of butts, attention to drainage, repair of bridges and boundary fences, combined with a persistent and unrelenting war against vermin occupy his time fully.

Foxes and crows are, without question, the major menace on a moor. One pair of foxes will assiduously work a moor and in the spring, when grouse are nesting, will destroy dozens of birds. Crows, too, will quarter back and forth searching for chicks or nests; on some moors the lesser and greater blackback gulls can be equally ruthless and must be destroyed whenever possible. Stoats, too, must be trapped, along with other ground vermin such as rats and weasels.

Few grouse shooters are perhaps aware of the amount of management and sheer hard slog necessary to show grouse across the line of butts. The smaller area of a low-ground shoot and the lack of equipment such as release pens and incubators tend to make you forget that, although he does not have to rear birds to supplement the wild stock, nevertheless the moor keeper finds himself fully occupied and moreover, dependent on elements outside his control for a successful season.

The one aspect of the moor with which the grouse shooter is intimately concerned is the lines of butts, used to conceal him from the birds. The traditional butt is a stone-built semi-circular construction lined with a drained stone base and topped with turves. The siting of a line of butts will be historical, taking into account the contours of the land and the traditional flight lines of the grouse. Such butts are elaborate and will doubtless be of a considerable age. Other forms of concealment may consist of a stone wall or a simple hurdle supported by two stakes, which can easily be shifted to take account of a change of wind or grouse habits.

There are few things worse on a grouse moor than an ill-constructed butt, too narrow or so badly drained that your feet are anchored in mud; nor should they be placed too close together or too far apart. The ideal is about 40 yards, though the topography may affect this.

A safe, comfortable butt will be about 4 feet square inside, and well packed with turves on the outside so that it merges with the ground. The floor will be lined with stone or wood and, if the latter, wire netting should be tacked down to prevent your slipping in wet weather. You should be able to raise or lower the turves on the rim to

Line of Guns walking up grouse

suit your height. In most cases there should be a wide vista fore and aft, but occasionally, due to the lie of the land, a butt may have only a 40- or 50-yard view in front, which means that birds will be on top of you abruptly.

It is a regrettable fact that accidents occur all too frequently on grouse moors when birds are being driven. Even experienced hands are caught out on occasion. Remember that this is an incredibly exciting sport, and for the beginner or novice it can also be a somewhat nerve-racking affair. The long pauses whilst the beaters or drivers work into position, the tendency to relax and then, suddenly, find the air filled with grouse, can catch out the unwary Gun. If he is not disciplined he may all too easily swing through the line of butts and fire at a bird between him and his nextdoor Gun. In a butt, the face is the most exposed part of the anatomy, and the chance of being blinded is high.

One may shoot *only* at birds in front or behind and when you turn to take a going-away bird, the gun must be raised to the high port position so that whilst transcribing an arc the barrels are always pointing at the sky. On many moors it is now the practice to place two sticks on either side of the butt to restrict the arc of fire and also force the shooter to raise his barrels when he turns round. Today, so many new faces appear each year on the moor that such a safety device is entirely justified.

Once the beaters are deemed to be within the danger zone, the keeper, or whoever is in charge of them, will sound a horn as a signal to the Guns that no further shots may be taken in front. Any Gun who does, in fact, take a potentially dangerous shot or who puts either his fellow-Guns or beaters at risk, should, without exception, be sent home immediately. Nothing is more calculated to ruin a day's sport than the knowledge that one of the Guns is a potential menace.

GUNS AND EQUIPMENT

The grouse moor is no place for automatic shotgun or pump-action gun. Anyone who ap-

Working a spaniel through thick bracken for grouse

pears with one of these monstrosities will politely – or not so politely! – be asked to retire. Side-by-side game guns are the ideal, though if you prefer an over-and-under, that is now acceptable. A light 12-bore side-by-side sidelock ejector, bored improved cylinder and half choke, firing a game load of 1 or 1⅛ oz is ideal. It is essential that the gun should fit you well and have sufficient life in it to swing quickly onto fast-moving close birds. It is a curious fact that whilst grouse are often shot close to the butts they are seldom, if ever, smashed.

Between drives always carry your guns in a well-padded gunslip; this will save the possibility of damage either in the cross-country vehicle or whilst walking. Moors are littered with stone and it is too easy to slip and dent the barrels.

Carry your cartridges in a capacious leather bag, capable of holding at least 100. There is nothing more infuriating than to run out of cartridges in the middle of a drive; you will incur the wrath of your host, quite apart from the unintended insult to expectations of sport. Make sure the bag has a broad strap. I also carry a cartridge belt fully loaded and replenish this from the bag, and lay out half a dozen cartridges

On a driven day the flanker's role is vital

111

on a convenient spot on the butt's rim. There are now available at least two types of cartridge belt from which the cartridges can be flipped out forwards rather than pulled up. This saves time and, as you will discover when birds are pouring at you in pack after pack – and it does happen! – time is a precious commodity. If you are shooting a moor where the bag is expected to be high, you may be supplied with a loader. He will undoubtedly know his job, but it is well for you both to have a dry run before the drive starts so that neither of you are fumbling. Don't forget to have a cartridge extractor about your person; with today's ammunition a jammed cartridge is unlikely, but be prepared. Waving a gun impotently at grouse streaming overhead could lead to a heart attack!

As far as clothing is concerned, there are three maxims to remember – camouflage, comfortable and waterproof. By camouflage I don't mean that you should adopt army-type smocks but that your clothing should blend with the surrounding shades of dark green and brown. Tweed is still the best, and the darker the colour, the better. A pair of plus-twos and a loose-fitting tweed jacket which can be shed under a hot August sun to reveal a dark green or brown shirt are ideal. Tweed is very nearly waterproof but if there is a chance of rain or mist, carry a thornproof of some sort. Top the whole collection with a dark cap or soft felt hat. I dislike tweed bonnets as they tend to shift when I look up for a high shot, the rear brim catching against my collar.

Footwear *must* be comfortable, waterproof and with some sort of serrated sole. A smooth-soled leather boot or shoe is a disaster as it tends to slip and slide on heather and grass. There is a wide selection on the market today and given the option I would choose a half-calf rubber boot, perhaps with some form of leather foot construction, or a supple leather ankle boot with a padded rim and sealed tongue. Whatever type of footwear you choose, be sure that it is well worn in. Blisters can ruin a day's sport.

If rain is in the offing, don't forget your towelling cravat to prevent water trickling down your neck and a light pair of overtrousers which can be slipped in your pocket or a sidebag.

A shooting stick is essential, not only as an aid to walking but to rest on in your butt and, again, there are numerous folding, collapsible, lightweight sticks on the market.

If you have a companion in your butt, make sure that he, or she, is equally as inconspicuous as you – no bright colours on the moor, please – and that he keeps out of sight and does not interfere with shooting. A well-trained helper can be of singular value in marking the slain and fallen. Marker cards can be obtained so that as birds drop round the butt their position can be fixed; this can save a great deal of time when picking up. If you have a dozen birds down, it is all too easy to forget their exact positions.

As far as dogs are concerned, in my view Guns have no business taking them on the moor. Your host will have arranged for a professional team of pickers-up who will be stationed behind the line of butts – and make sure you know exactly where they are – probably two or three hundred yards back. A pricked grouse will often carry on for a considerable distance before dropping and will only be noted by the picker-up. Your own dog cannot be placed in the butt as it is likely to get under your feet and may cause an accident, whilst the sound of the shots echoing around the stone walls will occasion it some distress. It must, therefore, be pegged outside the butt where, if it is light-coloured, it will have birds shying away from you. I repeat, unless you are picking-up, leave Fido at home.

THE DRIVE

You are now waiting quietly in your butt. You have checked your neighbouring Guns and know exactly where they lie and you have worked out your safety angles and zones of fire. You may have a wide vista in front and even be able to see the beaters as tiny specks a mile away, or you may have a slope in front and the first indication of grouse will be a whistle when a covey is on the wing before they burst into view.

You have loaded and now, despite the apparent peace and lack of movement, you must be prepared for action. Grouse have a knack of sliding forward, hugging the contours; don't

Gun's eye view of a driven covey

'I'm sure it fell there!'

Head keeper picking up at the end of a drive

expect them to come at you in a straight line. They may slant sideways, creep up the hill towards you, or perhaps gain height and sweep over like a cloud of starlings. Of one thing you can be certain, if you are new to the game you will be caught out by the first birds. The background is grouse-coloured and you really have to be attentive and acute to pick them up.

Watch out, too, for the old birds which, knowing the form, fly low, hugging the ground to drop into the heather short of the line of butts, then burst up at the last moment.

As far as style and shooting is concerned, Colonel John Standford put it succinctly in his book *Grouse Shooting* (Shooting Times Library) when he wrote:

It is almost impossible to teach any novice to shoot driven grouse any more than you could teach him to play a fast ball at cricket or lawn tennis. But certain things can be laid down. He must be able to move his feet quickly, which is not always the case in badly drained or constructed butts. I do not think it matters how he stands but he must keep still and be ready to raise his gun in an instant, and not talk politics with his loader or expect the latter to warn him when birds are approaching. Quickness in grouse shooting is everything. A very fine shot has advised that, when shooting, you should lean slightly forward with your weight on the left foot . . . and point your left hand at the bird and fire the instant your right hand has brought the butt home to your shoulder. If you can do that you need not bother your head with calculations about 'allowances'. A succession of grouse may be doing every speed from 30 to 50 miles an hour and you will usually find that the brain makes any allowance subconsciously. With a crossing shot it is a matter of a very short, very fast, swing. . . . With a few shots, e.g. the bird coming head high straight at you, you can put up the gun as if it was a rifle and fire straight at the bird, provided you do not dwell on the aim at all.

Of course, the experts have long claimed that the ideal is to take the first two birds well out in front, turn, change guns and knock out two behind. In practice it does not quite work like that! Taking the first bird well out in front sounds excellent advice, but to bring oneself to shoot at 50 yards calls for great strength of mind. In practice most birds are shot within 20 to 25 yards of the butt, some considerably less. Yet do not make the mistake of supposing that such birds will offer easy shots. Far from it. The popular press and the antis may bleat about birds 'being blasted from the sky by scatterguns', thus conjuring up an image of simple birds being virtually swatted out of the air, but the truth is very different. Anyone with such preconceived notions will find them rudely shattered on his first occasion in a butt.

It is a good idea to attend a clay-shooting school for a course of instruction before the season begins. Even the 'professionals' will top up their reactions with a short course. One of the finest shooting schools, Messrs Holland & Holland, whose ground lies near Northwood, Middlesex, have a series of artificial butts over which a wide variety of clays can be thrown linked to expert instruction.

Of one thing I can be certain. If you are fortunate enough to engage in a day's driven grouse shooting you will have experienced all that is best in shooting. The horizons, the broad vistas, the changing colours as great white clouds drift across the sky, the purple moor buzzing with the hum of bees, the scent of the heather, the whiff of burnt powder, the speeding, whir-ring flight of a pack of grouse over your butt and the recollection of a neat right-and-left in front will be with you when other memories of pheasant and partridge days have long since vanished.

SHOOTING SEASONS

These apply to England, Scotland and Wales as at September 1982 (all dates inclusive)

Grouse	12 August – 10 December
Partridge	1 September – 1 February
Pheasant	1 October – 1 February
Ptarmigan	12 August – 10 December
Blackgame	20 August – 10 December
Capercaillie	1 October – 31 January
Snipe	12 August – 31 January
Woodcock	1 October – 31 January
Scotland:	1 September – 31 January
Hares	No close season

Wild geese and duck
   In or over any
   area below high
   water mark (HWM)
   of ordinary
   spring tides   1 September – 20 February
   Elsewhere   1 September – 31 January

Golden plover   1 September – 31 January
(This is the
only wader that
may be shot)

Coot and moorhen   1 September – 31 January

Wildfowl that may be shot during the season are as follows:

Duck: Common Pochard, Gadwall, Goldeneye, Mallard, Pintail, Shoveler, Teal, Tufted, Wigeon

Geese: Canada, Greylag, Pinkfooted, Whitefront (Whitefront may be shot in England and Wales only)

Waders: Golden plover

Shooting on Sundays and Christmas Day is either prohibited or very restricted. The onus is on the individual to ascertain the exact position.

Deer

Species	Sex	England & Wales	Scotland
Red	Stags	1 August – 30 April	1 July – 20 October
	Hinds	1 November – 28 February	21 October – 15 February
Fallow	Buck	1 August – 30 April	1 August – 30 April
	Doe	1 November – 28 February	21 October – 15 February
Roe	Buck	1 April – 31 October	1 May – 20 October
	Doe	1 November – 28 February	21 October – 28 February
Sika	Stags	1 August – 30 April	1 August – 30 April
	Hinds	1 November – 28 February	21 October – 15 February

There is at present no statutory close season for muntjac or Chinese water deer, but the British Deer Society strongly recommends that there should be one from 1 March to 31 October.

Vermin   (for which there is no close season)

Birds: Collared Dove
                Crow
                Great Black-backed Gull
                Herring Gull
                Jackdaw
                Jay
                Lesser Black-backed Gull
                Magpie
                Pigeon (Feral)
                Rook
                Sparrow (House)
                Starling
                Woodpigeon
Mammals: Coypu
                Fox
                Mink
                Rabbit
                Rat (Brown)
                Squirrel (Grey)
                Stoat
                Weasel